Studio Suddo Neuve
Back to Earth —Urbanization without Depletion

Bauhaus Earth
Manuals

jovis

Foreword

by Alan Organschi and Philipp Misselwitz

By transforming the way we build, we might just save the planet.

Building as Disturbance

Building is a disruptive act. We tend to normalize its significant financial cost. We accept the temporary physical and logistical inconveniences at the building site and in its immediate surroundings and, if we're unfortunate enough to experience them, we tolerate the personal discomfort they may cause. But we tend to ignore the broader social dislocation and disenfranchisement that building can create and we almost never see or experience—much less assess and account for—the even more remote environmental impacts of the construction process.

Beyond those specific boundaries of the building site and its adjacent spatial and socioeconomic contexts, the act of building has deep and unsettlingly adverse effects: the disturbance of source landscapes and ecosystems, the consumption of rapidly diminishing material and energy resources, the emission of heat-trapping atmospheric gasses, and the steady accretion of waste across the planet's surface that can be directly tied to the physical artifacts we create and use. An open-pit copper mine, an extensive forest clearcut, a toxic brownfield, a leaching landfill, a sprawling suburban tract can serve only as proxies for all the unseen consequences of our activities as builders. If we were to further pry apart the links in the vast supply chains that answer our demand for building products, we would find the exploitation of workers and worse, practices of human

1 Global Alliance for Buildings and Construction, International Energy Agency and the United Nations Environment Programme, "2019 Global Status Report for Buildings and Construction," 2019, 41.

2 Callun Keith Purchase et al., "Circular Economy of Construction and Demolition Waste: A Literature Review on Lessons, Challenges, and Benefits," *Materials* 15, no. 1 (December 23, 2021): 76.

3 Guillaume Habert et al. "Carbon Budgets for Buildings: Harmonising Temporal, Spatial and Sectoral Dimensions." *Buildings & Cities* 1, no. 1 (July 1, 2020).

indenture or slavery. Habitats destroyed, species extinguished, water and **soil** fouled, and, to an even less visible degree, an alarming increase in atmospheric concentrations of carbon dioxide are the merely anecdotal record of the human behaviors that have pushed us past a sustainable threshold of planetary habitability. This is the legacy of our extractive building economy.

Most of us are by now well aware of how the extraction and combustion of fossil fuels and the associated emission of greenhouse gasses result in the warming of the atmosphere. It is only very recently, however, that we have come to acknowledge that the global building sector—all the industrial activity and infrastructural artifacts associated with the materialization, operation, and ultimately disposal of the constructed environments in which we live and work—bears a significant share of responsibility for the sum of anthropogenic impacts that have brought us to this critical juncture in the story of our own species and those other organisms that inhabit the planet with us.

Conservatively measured across the building life cycle, the construction sector's emissions of carbon dioxide and its equivalents represent about 39 percent of annual anthropogenic contributions to climate change.[1] The production phase of that life cycle consumes 84 percent of all minerals excavated by the global mining industry and produces 30 percent of waste.[2] With 2.5 billion additional people slated to inhabit global cities by 2050, the environmental consequences of our business-as-usual materials, means, and methods of producing buildings and infrastructure will grow in direct proportion to our consumption of the raw material and energy required to meet the massive demand for housing alone. By mid-century, this anticipated boom in building will have devoured more than two thirds of our remaining terrestrial carbon budget.[3] Meanwhile, given our recent record, it seems likely that other critical objectives of sustainability—promoting social equity, environmental restoration, and economic feasibility—will remain largely unaddressed.

Our Bauhaus Earth

As architects, planners, and builders working at the core of this planetary crisis, we must embrace our agency in reinventing the act of building as an instrument of terrestrial healing and regeneration. We are, after all, the specifiers of material and technique in the manufacture, operation, and disposal of the largest and most durable artifacts that the human species produces and that comprise an outsize share of our current habitat.

History has shown how this agency can be mobilized. A little over a century ago, a new institution and novel pedagogy, the Staatliches Bauhaus, was founded in Weimar, Germany. The Bauhaus sought to bring together practitioners, teachers, and students from the increasingly interdependent disciplines of architecture, artisanry, industry, and the visual and performing arts. Thinking through making and radical experimentation in design and manufacture was to inspire a new vision for an urbanizing world that had only just experienced the cataclysmic destruction of the World War I. The Bauhaus became the epicenter of Europe's artistic and architectural creativity and was to become an inspirational reference for subsequent generations of designers and builders seeking novel means to create new forms, rebalance social hierarchies, and redistribute economic opportunity. Today, the historic Bauhaus is still revered for its radical approach, but we also acknowledge that its lessons are implicated in the deeply problematic legacy of modernist building and planning and, by extension, their extractive economic practices and their destructive impacts to our planetary systems.

Almost exactly one hundred years later, on Earth Day 2021, **Bauhaus Earth** was founded to address—through the integration of scientific analysis and building experimentation—that more troubling legacy of the original Bauhaus and, more fundamentally, the responsibility of the global building sector for the dire environmental and social challenges that humankind now faces. As a counterfactual scenario, might the activities and artifacts of the building life cycle and the processes of urbanization serve as a force for eco-systemic repair and climate restoration rather than one of predation and waste? The sheer scale of our consumption of material and energy in the formation of human settlement suggests that the transformation of our tools and techniques of impact assessment, our means and methods of construction, our models of building finance, our frameworks for resource governance, and our modes of environmental advocacy might offer us a significant lever in the fight against climate change and biodiversity loss. How we go about transforming these processes, engaging citizens as well as society's professional classes, reforming building practice, and reengaging our cities as vital contributors to social and environmental restoration remains the essential question.

Building for Environmental Regeneration and Social Equity

To answer this question and catalyze the kinds of material and methodological experimentation and social action that will be a fundamental part of deep and durable change, we offer this series of instruction manuals for anyone whose work touches upon the sequence of activities that comprise the life cycle of buildings and growth of cities. The purpose of an instruction **manual** is to identify and articulate a problem, to outline the process of solving it, to enumerate the materials, tools, and techniques required and to offer along with them a few tricks of the trade to guide the reader past the inevitable pitfalls and barriers that might present themselves in even the simplest and most seemingly straightforward operations.

The specific topics addressed by each of the *Bauhaus Earth Manuals* represent different angles of approach to the technical transformation of global building and the establishment of the regulatory, political, educational, and economic contexts and conditions that will ensure that change is appropriately rapid, effective, and long lasting. Taken individually, each manual seeks to describe a specific subject and state-of-the-art practice in what must ultimately become a collective effort to mitigate and possibly even reverse the steady destabilization of the planet's systems by the currently linear economic paradigms of building manufacture, operation, and demolition. The *Bauhaus Earth Manuals* are not prescriptions but rather demonstrations of potential approaches and testbeds of practice that will inevitably evolve through continual iteration, revision, adaptation, and refinement by like-minded participants in the struggle for system change. The unique structure of the *Bauhaus Earth Manuals* aims to bridge big-picture analysis of building in a changing climate (Provocation & Intervention) with hands-on, replicable instructions for implementation (Manual & Outcomes). The inclusion of interviews (Voices) allows for the representation of a broad spectrum of actors in this series. A sister series, the *Bauhaus Earth Essays,* features the critical voices in ongoing theoretical discourses that serve as conceptual inspiration and build the philosophical infrastructure for the regenerative transformation of our cities and planet.

This first *Bauhaus Earth Manual, Back to Earth,* focuses on the development of an alternative building element that could make a critical impact also in non-forested or forest-critical regions: the unfired earth block. The goal of the Senegal-based collective is to counteract the socioeconomic realignments and dramatic atmospheric impacts associated with the increasingly reflexive use of cast-in-place concrete and cementitious blocks in the region.

Through a rigorous process of soil analysis, component testing, and assembly prototyping, the *Back to Earth* block designers demonstrate the feasibility of creating construction components with negligible greenhouse gas emissions in a low-tech context. The transparent assessment, precise mapping, and meticulous accounting of *Back to Earth* is an important contribution to the broader debate on the relationship of construction and climate change, seeking to inspire new experimentation in the field of earth-based construction. As a work in progress, it invites like-minded researchers and makers to engage with, and then challenge or adapt, its ideas, objectives, and techniques.

Mako, Senegal (2017–25)

Observations on Earth

Asphalt and concrete are covering Earth,[4] so much so that the weight of anthropogenic mass is now exceeding the mass of all living matter on the planet.[5] Our culture of extractivism has long forgotten the underlying cycles and processes that create(d) and maintain(ed) Earth as a habitat. Instead of conserving and caring, we treat Earth as an inexhaustible resource and transform its outer crust into single life-cycle products. The planet's health is thereby intrinsically linked to our treatment of earth, the substance that makes up its land surface. While desertification due to deforestation, soil acidification due to agricultural mismanagement, and contamination due to chemical spillages and waste disposal are indicative of the irreparable mistreatment, the link between human habitat, earth, and Earth remains underexplored.

Once the most universally used building material, earth has been replaced by concrete, steel, and plastic. We view the vanishing of earth from the built environment as representative of the loss of a connection to our planet Earth. Transforming the minerals that make up E/earth into infinitely bound composites interferes with the natural processes of sedimentation and rock formation with unpredictable consequences.[6] Foregoing earth for unrecyclable materials therefore decimates the natural rock cycle and thereby Earth systems.

4 Throughout the book we distinguish between our planet Earth (capitalized) and earth (lowercase) when we speak of soil.

5 Emily Elhacham et al., "Global Human-Made Mass Exceeds All Living Biomass," *Nature* 588, no. 7838 (December 2020): 442–44.

6 Hengfeng Liu et al., "Environmental Behavior of Construction and Demolition Waste as Recycled Aggregates for Backfilling in Mines: Leaching Toxicity and Surface Subsidence Studies," *Journal of Hazardous Materials* 389 (May 5, 2020).

●1 Earth Masonry in Construction

For years, we have been questioning the replacement of earth architecture with concrete buildings and have sought regenerative building solutions that could **re-entangle** human habitats and the natural environment in their materiality. *Back to Earth* documents an attempt to revitalize earth as a building material and to scale our impact back to **planetary boundaries**. It illustrates the negotiations of contemporary pressures of urbanization, capital, and labor with the reintroduction of earth-based materials to the construction sites of Senegal. *Back to Earth* thereby turns away from the typical, picturesque documentation of architectural projects in a country of the Global South, financed through donations of Western organizations and governments. Rather, this manual reflects our experience of working with earth-based materials and crafting building components that are reactive to material and climate. We challenge the status quo of reinforced concrete buildings replacing **vernacular architecture** without consideration or reinterpretation of the latter's principles and materials. As seemingly mundane as the replacement of traditional building materials with concrete and steel may seem, it epitomizes the disentanglement of humans and the natural environment. Our work seeks to respond to the conditions of local ecosystems and to counteract the disintegration of local building cultures by the globalized and universalized principles of modernity. Our goal, with this publication, is to provide the necessary details for the adaptation and replication of a socially, economically, and environmentally viable alternative to concrete architecture in other places. In this (re-)discovery of climate-adaptive choices in form and materiality, we underline the importance of a holistic understanding of the impact throughout the life cycles of the materials we manufacture and the buildings we build. ●1

Back to Earth

We realized that achieving these objectives requires working on multiple disciplines and scales, and that our work as architects and builders would not start with a floor plan or an elevation but with studies and experiments. While it was clear that in the long run demonstration buildings would be a key lever of our **intervention** into the local building industry, our work started with identifying and sourcing regionally available building materials, and exploring their particularities, strengths, and shortcomings. Rather than taking measures of a building site, our work started with experimentation, prototyping, and embracing an iterative and sometimes frustrating learning process.

Since 2017, we have established a comprehensive practice for material research, manufacturing, design, and construction that emphasizes a holistic approach to responsible architecture in the process of urbanization. We come together in different constellations under the name of Studio Suddo Neuve. Suddo Neuve, which roughly translates to *new house* from **Pulaar** and **French**, signals the objective of our architectural intervention to coin a new materiality for contemporary architecture in the region. As we aimed for systemic impact rather than the creation of a single exemplary architectural object, we created organizational frameworks and built the necessary infrastructure to replicate research findings and offer them at a competitive price. And while this endeavor started as an NGO, it has now diversified into a design studio and building-material manufacturing company with a permanent production site. Throughout the years of our work, we have sought exposure to craftspeople, builders, political stakeholders, and the broader community, facilitating the dissemination of our findings locally. Seven years into this work, this book is the last act of our intervention, and the attempt to make our knowledge accessible beyond Mako. ●2

Back to Earth is an accumulation of conversations with architects experienced in building with earth, earth-block and block-press manufacturers, masons who have worked with the material on construction sites, and the users and residents of earth architecture paired with our personal experience of developing and building with earth blocks in Mako. In this sense, we view this manual as a collective endeavor, enriched by the existing network of experts and their willingness to openly share their knowledge. Additionally, we draw from project documentations, earth building manuals, and scientific publications to complement our experiential knowledge and deduce more universally applicable insights.

We observed that the resources available often emphasized specific aspects rather than providing a comprehensive guide for earth-block architecture, either focusing on the production of materials or the finished buildings but rarely on the components and

●2 Timeline of Intervention

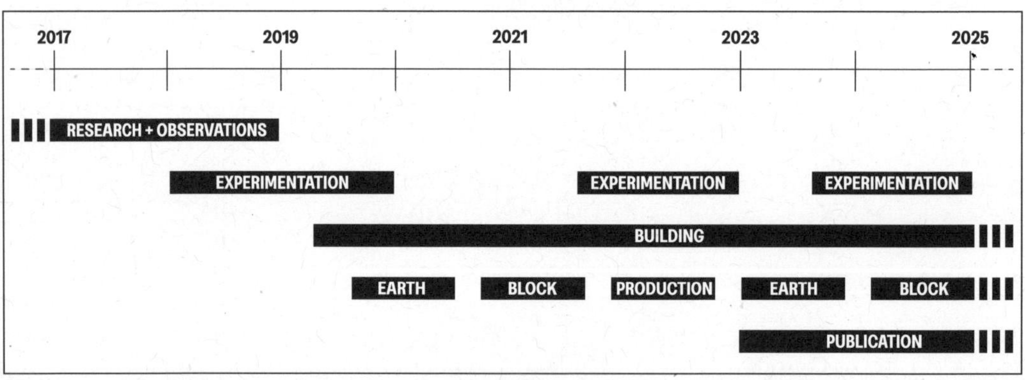

assemblies. Recognizing the missing documentation of earth-based building processes and the intrinsic link between the manufacturing of materials and the act of building, we embarked on an effort to holistically integrate and synthesize our insights. Therefore, the manual spans across the realms of material experimentation, manufacturing, design, and construction, progressing from the microscale examination of clay minerals and the unit of an earth block to the assembly of masonry, and the integration with other building materials for architectural production. Ultimately, it aims to understand these elements in regards to their broader urban and natural environment and to evaluate their social, ecological, and economic impact. *Back to Earth* is not confined to the showcasing of a chronology of completed projects but a reorganization of our work to showcase a replicable systemic shift in a local material and building culture. We hope to draw attention to the need for a more regenerative architecture and to offer a tangible starting point that can be activated in built environments around the globe.

Provocation

Cementing the West African City

Eccentric in form and monumental in materiality, the buildings from the post-independence period characterize the urban landscapes of **West Africa**. They stand as arches, pyramids, rectangles, and ellipses around national squares, educational campuses, and fairgrounds, in clear geometrical forms that dominate their surroundings and manifest an interpretation of modernism unseen in the West. Buildings like the headquarters of the Central Bank of West African States (BCEAO) in Dakar, Senegal, the Ghanaian National Museum in Accra, and the mixed-use building La Pyramide in Abidjan, Ivory Coast, reflect a synthesis of **International Style** and local vernacular form. While some of the buildings are now in decay, they are important markers of architectural history in the city making of West Africa. ●3

Between 1957 and 1961, twelve of the sixteen West African countries became independent from European colonial rule and embarked on a quest of nation building. While the liberalization from imperialism is particular to every country and the extent of decolonization can rightfully be questioned, the construction of new national identities was central to these West African countries in the decades following independence. The architecture of this time embodies the efforts to build national identities independent from the colonizers.

●3 BCEAO Building in Dakar, Senegal

Architecture and urbanism were deployed as tools to contrast the present from the past and to signal progress to the world. The International Style was the style of choice, seen as the access point to the global playing field of trade, politics, and culture.[7] In opposition to the built heritage of colonial times that evoked an immediate connection to a particular European country, International Modernism seemingly offered an identity without a direct link to the Western metropolis; its universal ideals promised an untainted expression of progress and an integration into the global order, as had been demonstrated in the Brasilia, Brazil, and in Chandigarh, India, in the late nineteen-fifties. These ideals were so central to African leaders that, during the two decades following the wave of independence, public spending on buildings was three times higher in West Africa than on transport infrastructure; in the decades before, the opposite was true.[8] Governments even ordered the demolition of vernacular architecture, replacing it with buildings built from industrial materials to showcase the aspired prosperity to citizens and internationals alike.[9] The decoloniality of the erected buildings has been relativized by multiple scholars, who have traced the influence of European architects and architecture schools on African Modernism and have deemed some of the buildings mere testing grounds for architectural experimentation by European expatriates.[10] While the originality of the derived architectural languages differ case by case and remain a point of contestation, the conditions of the architectural production and the materiality were unequivocally identical copies of the Western precedent of modern architecture, reflected in the widespread use of manually processed concrete.[11]

As do the aforementioned buildings of African independence: they took no inspiration from local materials but instead were liberated from material constraints through international supply chains and technological development. Modernity's affinity for reinforced concrete is thereby characterized by its flexibility regarding form and high structural performance. The absence of a genius loci, which modernism rationalizes with its claim of universality, translates to an indifference to the natural environment and evokes a distancing of man from nature and of material sources from the construction sites where the materials are employed. Today, this materiality does not contrast with the surrounding urban landscape anymore. Rather the aesthetics of concrete surfaces are so ubiquitous in the West African city that the material becomes almost invisible. However, when these buildings were constructed in the nineteen-seventies, they "Africanized" the use of concrete by detaching the notion of coloniality from the material.[12]

7 Manuel Herz, et al., eds., *African Modernism: The Architecture of Independence: Ghana, Senegal, Côte d'Ivoire, Kenya, Zambia* (Zurich: Park Books, 2015).

8 Diala Toure, *Créations architecturales et artistiques en Afrique sub-saharienne (1948–1995): Bureaux d'études Henri Chomette* (Paris: L'Harmattan, 2002), 66.

9 Labelle Prussin, "The Anthropology of Architecture and the Architecture of Anthropology," in *Architectures of Belonging: Inhabiting Worlds in Rural West Africa*, ed. Ann Cassiman (Antwerp: BAI Pub, 2011), 22.

10 Łukasz Stanek, *Architecture in Global Socialism: Eastern Europe, West Africa, and the Middle East in the Cold War* (Princeton: Princeton University Press, 2020).

11 Now, sixty years later, the influence of the West is receding, and Chinese foreign direct investment is leaving its marks on the architecture and cityscapes of West African countries. For example, in 2018 the Museum of Black Civilization was opened to much fanfare in Dakar, Senegal. The museum was celebrated for its potential ability to rewrite historical narratives and can broadly be seen as a concrete expression of the new epistemology that independence brought for the Global South. However, a visit to the museum reveals that the $30 mio. China invested into the museum have left their trace. The monumental entrance of the museum features a small, but poignant "China Aid" sign and the exhibitions draw links to Chinese culture.

12 Armelle Choplin, "Cementing Africa: Cement Flows and City-Making along the West African Corridor (Accra, Lomé, Cotonou, Lagos)," *Urban Studies* 57, no. 9 (July 2020): 1982.

Urbanization and Depletion

In the fifty years following, concrete took over West Africa; dubbed the "grey gold," the mix of **cement**, aggregates, and water grew beyond the construction sites and entered the realms of politics and culture; the price of a bag of cement has become an economic indicator and it is gifted at special occasions such as marriages and retirements.[13] Fifty-kilogram bags of cement can be purchased in the most remote places; small rural shops offer cement along with basic food items, such as rice and cooking oil. As a result, the borrow pits where raw earth was sourced, and the forests where bamboo was cultivated have been abandoned, and the richest man in Africa—Aliko Dangote—is the founder of a cement-producing company with a production capacity of more than fifty million tons annually in ten sub-Saharan African countries.[14]

This "cementing" and expansion of West Africa's urban environments reflect the globally prevailing amensalism of humans and their natural environments, in which the production of habitable spaces is conditioned by the clearcutting of forests, the unrestrained extraction of resources, and the continuous sealing of surfaces.[15] The prioritization of industrial efficiency and short-term economic gains over planetary health and individual well-being have rendered the construction of built environments into an ecological and social crisis. In the West African city, concrete epitomizes this destruction of the natural environment due to its uncontested monopoly as a construction material and the overwhelmingly negative ecological impacts throughout its life cycle. Sourcing the base materials of concrete—sand and gravel as aggregates and limestone as the binder—from quarries devastates landscapes. Following the physical decimation of natural environments through this extractivism, the production and transportation of concrete (and its composite materials) are carbon-intensive, translating into a significant impact on the planet's atmosphere. In 2021, cement alone accounted for 28 percent of all embodied carbon of the construction sector globally, with more than 80 percent of this share produced in the Global South.[16] While projections suggest that high-income regions will see a decrease in construction-related emissions due to the possibility of meeting shifting demands for architecture with the repurposing of existing built structures and decarbonizing the energy grid, West Africa will require a significant amount of new construction to meet the growing population's demand for living space, especially in urban environments.

West Africa's population multiplied five-fold between 1950 and 2015, and its current population

13 Choplin, "Cementing Africa," 1978.

14 Moshood Ademola Fayemiwo and Margie Marie Neal, *Aliko Mohammad Dangote: The Biography of the Richest Black Person in the World*, first edition (Houston, TX: Strategic Book Publishing and Rights Co, 2013); Ehiedu E. G. Iweriebor, *Dangote and Pan-Africa Economic Transformation: The Revolutionary Impact* (Bodija, Ibadan: Bookbuilders-Editions Africa, 2018).

15 Maha Salman, "Sustainability and Vernacular Architecture: Rethinking What Identity Is," in *Urban and Architectural Heritage Conservation within Sustainability*, ed. Kabila Hmood (2019).

16 United Nations Environment Programme and Yale Center for Ecosystems + Architecture, *Building Materials and the Climate: Constructing a New Future* (Nairobi, 2023): 7, https://wedocs.unep.org/xmlui/handle/20.500.11822/43293, last accessed September 23, 2024.

growth rate of 2.5 percent is the second highest in the world.[17] Of its current 440 million people (2023) only 50 percent live in cities, which translates into a growth potential that will see the urban population more than double by 2050 to more than 515 million people.[18] These anticipated high rates of urbanization will not only result in the growth of existing metropolitan areas but will also see the construction of entirely new metropolises in the region. Projections indicate that these conglomerations will not exclusively be formed on the coast but also in the Sahelian Corridor, a stretch of savanna land that lies between the Sahara Desert in the north and forest land in the south.[19] ●4

The potentials and challenges this immense population growth brings have been widely discussed. However, the material impact of housing another billion people is often overlooked in these discussions. If this rapid population growth in the Sahel region continues to be addressed with concrete-centric architecture, any other effort to reduce greenhouse gas emissions globally will be nullified by the increased ecological footprint of this building effort alone. The architecture that meets the current demands has lost the ambition of the pioneer buildings from the nineteen-seventies and retreated to simple copies of Western concrete typologies. Only cement and corrugated sheet metal, which exist independent of local construction materials, seem to be able to cater to the population growth within the current economic paradigms. Neither local, social, and climatic circumstances nor vernacular architecture and building techniques have been considered in the search for adequate typologies and materials for the West African urbanization.

The steep population increase in the region is therefore directly correlated to a similarly strong increase in the demand for cement. While the Covid-19 pandemic has had a significant effect on the cement market in West Africa, with prices rising due to transportation shortages, the industry experienced growth rates of 5 to 6 percent in the years prior. In 2023, the market recovered with an annual output of 43.6 million tons and an expected growth rate of 6.2 percent.[20] This number is two times higher than the global market growth and particularly interesting because West Africa's annual GDP-per-capita growth rate has been stagnant since 2015.[21] A closer look at specific economies in West Africa confirms that per-capita cement consumption is correlated to population growth and not GDP. The economies of Nigeria, Senegal, and Togo suggest such a trend, where even in times of economic stagnation or decline, the per-capita cement consumption increased. Although the West Africa per-capita annual consumption of cement

17 United Nations, Department of Economic and Social Affairs, *World Population Prospects 2022: Summary of Results*, Statistical Papers—United Nations (Ser. A), Population and Vital Statistics Report (August 2022).

18 United Nations, *World Population Prospects 2022*.

19 OECD and Sahel and West Africa Club, *Africa's Urbanisation Dynamics 2020: Africapolis, Mapping a New Urban Geography*, West African Studies (2020).

20 IMARC Group, "West Africa Cement Market Report by Type, End Use, and Country 2024–2032)," (2023), https://www.imarcgroup.com/west-africa-cement-market, last accessed July 8, 2024; IMARC Group, "Cement Market Report by Type, End Use, and Region (2024–2032)," (2023), https://www.imarcgroup.com/cement-manufacturing-plant, last accessed July 8, 2024.

21 African Development Bank, "African Development Bank Statistical Data Portal," (December 2023), https://dataportal.opendataforafrica.org/, last accessed July 8, 2024.

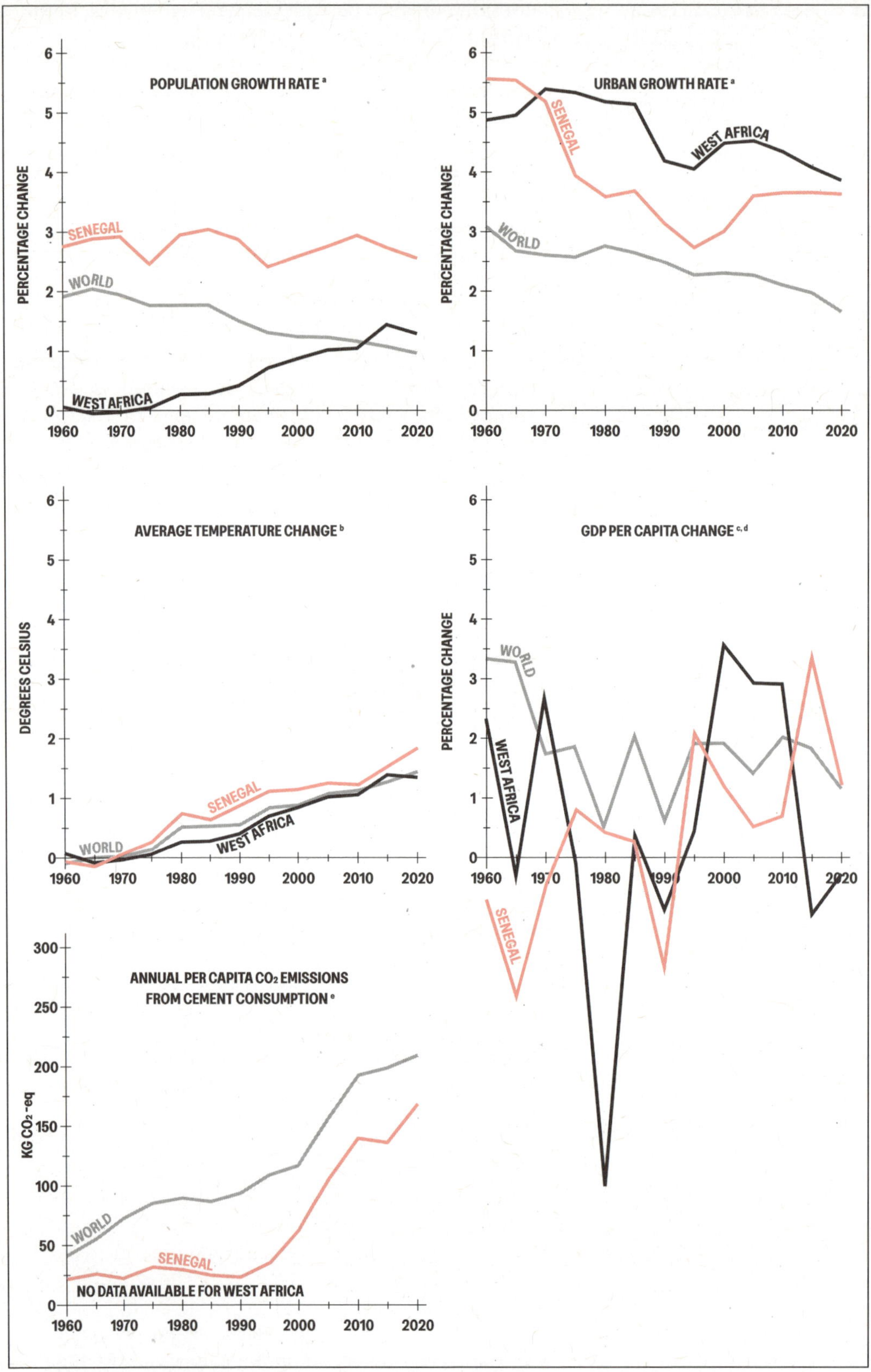

●4 Indicators of Change. (Urban) Population, GDP, Cement-Related CO_2 Emissions, and Temperature (→ p. 134)

of 145 kilograms is currently far below the global average of 549 kilograms, the prospects of a growing population that increases its cement consumption despite the absence of significant economic stimulus is alarming, especially given that cement price levels in the region remain 200 percent above the global average.[22] Africa is therefore seen as the "last great cement frontier" and has seen significant amounts of investment in the concrete industry over recent years.[23] Notably, European companies such as the Vicat Group (France), Heidelberg Materials (Germany), and the Holcim Group (Switzerland) have been establishing cement plants in West Africa, strongly reducing cement imports from other regions. At the same time, the presence of these international companies is causing profits to flow back to the Western metropolis rather than staying local, entangling West Africa into a global economy of building materials.

The prospect of ever-growing cement consumption and production in West Africa poses a considerable challenge to the effort of reducing global greenhouse gas emissions. Cement's carbon footprint is extremely high due to the energy required to induce the endothermic reaction that transforms clinker ($CaCO_3$) into decomposed oxides (CaO). Globally, fossil fuels are most commonly used to fire the clinker. However, even in a scenario where renewable energy carriers are used in the process, carbon dioxide emissions will remain high due to the direct emission of carbon dioxide from the carbonate. According to generic life-cycle assessment data sets for the production of cement (A1–A3), during the reaction each ton produced emits the equivalent of 813 kilograms of carbon dioxide into the atmosphere; this calculation does not account for the additional carbon dioxide emitted by transportation and the extraction of the aggregates needed to produce concrete.[24] Of the 813 kilograms of carbon dioxide emitted in the production of one ton of cement, approximately 37.5 percent are emitted through the combustion of fuels, while the larger portion is emitted as a by-product of the reaction.[25]

If the projections hold true and the region's cement consumption continues its growth rates of at least 5 percent per year, then the annual consumption of cement per capita will rise to 470 kilograms in the next twenty-five years ($A = P\ (1 + r/n)^{(nt)}$). If population growth rates also follow their predictions, then the 800 million people living in West Africa by 2050 will consume a total of 376 million tons in that year, emitting 305 million tons of carbon dioxide in its production alone.

In this scenario, total building-material-related greenhouse gas emissions will increase by an average of 0.7 percent per year, to 4.6 gigatons of carbon-dioxide equivalents per year in 2060.[26] Scientists estimate

22 Tradeship Publications Ltd, *The Global Cement Report*, 14th ed. (Surrey, 2021); Bruce Byiers, Karim Karaki, and Jan Vanheukelom, "Regional Markets, Politics and Value Chains: The Case of West African Cement," *European Centre for Development Policy Management*, no. 216 (September 2017).

23 Lyal White, "The Case of Cement," in *Africans Investing in Africa: Understanding Business and Trade, Sector by Sector*, ed. Terence McNamee, Mark Pearson, and Wiebe Boer (London: Palgrave Macmillan UK, 2015), 124–46.

24 Sphera Solutions GmbH, "Cement (CEM II 32,5)" (Ökobaudat, 2022), https://oekobaudat.de/OEKOBAU.DAT/datasetdetail/process.xhtml?uuid=55af842c-7d33-4d0c-b33b-ac7564e573bf&version=20.23.050&stock=OBD_2023_I&lang=de/, last accessed July 8, 2024.

25 International Energy Agency, *Energy Technology Perspectives 2016: Towards Sustainable Urban Energy Systems* (June 2016), https://www.iea.org/reports/energy-technology-perspectives-2016, last accessed September 23, 2024.

26 Xiaoyang Zhong et al., "Global Greenhouse Gas Emissions from Residential and Commercial Building Materials and Mitigation Strategies to 2060," *Nature Communications* 12, no. 1 (October 21, 2021): 2.

27 Steve Smith et al., *The State of Carbon Dioxide Removal*, 2nd Edition (2024).

28 Agence Française de Développement, "Cement, Confronting Ecological Responsibility and Economic Imperatives" (May 2011), https://www.proparco.fr/en/ressources/cement-confronting-ecological-responsibility-and-economic-imperatives, last accessed September 23, 2024.

that 10 gigatons of carbon dioxide need to be removed from the atmosphere each year to keep with target of limiting global warming to 1.5 degrees Celsius. In a business-as-usual scenario West African cement production alone would make up 2.6 percent of this budget.[27] These predictions seem daunting but they are central in understanding the seriousness of the current climate disaster and in targeting the right root causes. Reducing the amount of cement will be crucial to achieve the climate targets, especially as the life cycle of cement also leads to further ecological impacts through its non-biodegradability and irreversible binding of aggregates.

Typologies in Transition

The popularity of concrete can largely be attributed to its affordability, structural stability, and low-tech application. But the shift in materiality to concrete also indicates a stronger specialization of societies. While vernacular architecture is most often constructed by its future inhabitants, concrete construction is shaped by the processes of service societies. Due to its versatility, concrete is used in buildings as well as in infrastructure such as sanitation systems, roadbeds, and pavements. Especially for infrastructure and sewage systems, the alternatives for concrete are limited to non-existent. Hence, it is illusionary to demand a reduction of concrete consumption to zero. However, there are viable alternatives to concrete in many other applications. Especially in West Africa, concrete has been used for its ease of application rather than with material sophistication and adaptation, leading to the highly ineffective usage of a material with a significant environmental cost. A study by the French Development Agency (L'Agence française de développement—AFD) shows that especially in emerging markets the construction of new housing represents the largest consumption of cement, while economies of the Global North use a larger share of cement in infrastructure projects.[28] ●5 A reduction of the amount of concrete used in the housing sector could hence have a very significant impact on overall cement consumption, while avoiding an impedi-

●5 Proportion of Concrete Used for the Construction of Residential Buildings and Housing in Reference to Total Building Volume ***(→ p. 134)***

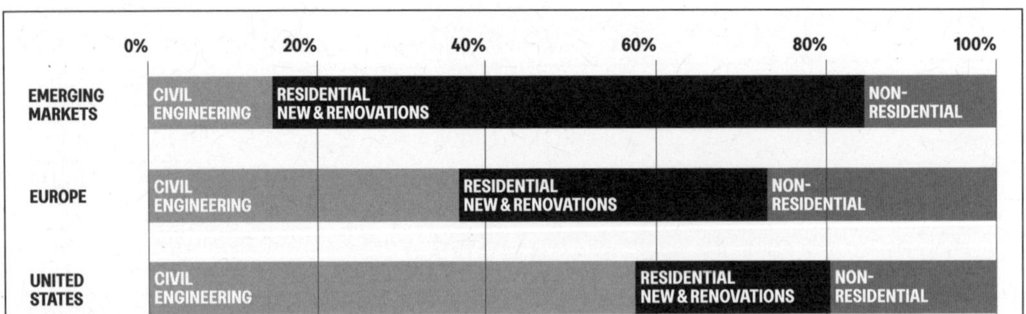

ment of progress through the restrictive use of concrete for infrastructure.

Zooming in on Senegal, the western-most African country and the place where we work, the transformation of local typologies through the introduction of concrete as a new materiality is particularly evident. The inflated use of concrete becomes especially clear when observing the evolution of housing architecture in smaller towns and rural villages. Next to round earth huts with thatched roofs, multistory cinderblock houses are rising into the air. Most houses are neither clay huts nor multistory concrete houses, but hybrids that can be seen as a snapshot of this transition, a physically manifestation of the evolution in architecture that exhibits how material and form have changed in the past two decades.

The first iteration in this transformation simply substitutes the cob work or sun-dried adobe bricks for concrete blocks and the thatched roof for corrugated sheet metal. The rectangular blocks encourage the construction of rectangular shapes, so the hut is no longer circular. However, in terms of floor area and functionality the concrete copy is identical to its vernacular predecessor, even mimicking the clustering of the round huts.

The concrete hut further evolved into the family bungalow that consists of two to four bedrooms connected by a central hallway. The design saves wall surfaces by having a linear design, as such it can be understood as a line of concrete huts. However, bathrooms and cooking facilities are located in smaller buildings or ephemeral structures in the backyards. More recently, bungalows have enlarged their built space to include larger rooms that can also house interior communal spaces. In addition to the concrete blocks, this transformation phase also includes the use of reinforced concrete columns and ring anchors to ensure the stability of the structures. As buildings increase in size, their relationship to the neighborhood changes. They tend to shift their orientation toward road and pathway access points, moving away from courtyards.

In their densest iteration, the concrete buildings are built with a concrete celling and with more than one floor. The main entrance is located on the road, and bathrooms and plumbing are incorporated into the building. Additional communal space is created through a roof terrace. However, as the interior communal space is limited to one room and the courtyard no longer exists, large gatherings, such as weddings or baptisms are moved to the adjoining streets, which transform into an extension of the private space for special events. The visible evolution of architecture points toward a demand of increased density achieved by larger and multistory buildings. In most towns, the impetus of concrete

29 For further discussion and analysis of urban typologies in West Africa, see Mae-ling Lokko et al., "Comparing the Whole Life Cycle Carbon Impact of Conventional and Biogenic Building Materials across Major Residential Typologies in Ghana and Senegal," *Sustainable Cities and Society* 106 (July 2024).

architecture seems to be radiating from the main road, with multistory construction concentrated along the main transport access points and being virtually absent in the neighborhoods and periphery.[29] ●6

This trend toward a cemented residential architecture is manifesting itself throughout the West African region, replacing the diverse and culturally specific vernacular architecture with the universal concrete house. This shift seems logical at first, as concrete does not require much skilled labor but creates a building industry of suppliers and laborers around itself. Concrete also allows for the construction of multistory buildings, which is unachievable with most traditional building techniques, but necessary in increasingly densely populated areas. Based on the belief that only concrete can cater to contemporary architectural needs, the materiality and form of the modern buildings exist independent of a critical understanding of local typologies and materials. ●7

On closer inspection, however, the construction with concrete blocks can not only be criticized from a global climate perspective but also has resulted in new, previously unknown problems at the local level. In addition to high costs and the loss of local funds to global corporations, the material and construction technique are not suitable for the local climate. The concrete houses overheat during the dry season, making their communal spaces, at best, uncomfortable and, at worst, unuseable. Similarly, the construction with cement requires large quantities of sand. Local soils are not suitable as aggregates for concrete construction. The demand for sand, sourced from riverbeds and pit mines, has led to erosion, the destruction of ecosystems, and even the formation of criminal networks that illegally source aggregates in Senegal.

Between Memory and Invention

In our view, the inefficient use of concrete and its poor adaptation to local circumstances can largely be attributed to a disproportionally slow improvement

●6 Evolution of Housing Typologies in Senegal

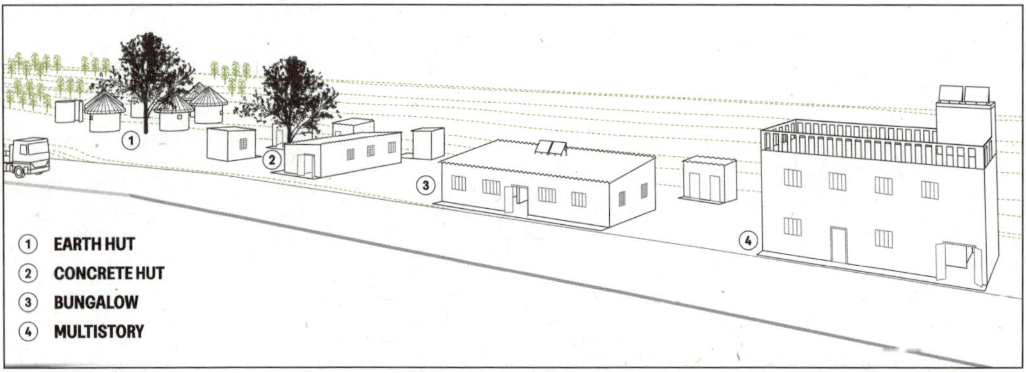

●7 Material Change from Adobe to Concrete Block

of building trades and construction equipment. The bare availability of cement has not significantly impacted the technical construction conditions and has therefore sustained the culture of an architecture without architects and a construction site without significant mechanical support. On most construction sites the concrete is mixed by hand and transported in buckets. Straight and even planks for formworks are a rarity, and scaffolding is in most cases improvised with bamboo and oil barrels. This infrastructural gap has only allowed for the emergence of low-skill specialized labor, such as brickmakers, masons, and painters, who build buildings as simple frame-and-infill constructions that underutilize reinforced concrete's structural capabilities. ●8

Climate change, urbanization, and societal specialization demand a rethinking of the reactionary concrete architecture and seek a building typology and materiality that reconsiders locality yet can cater to contemporary demands. However, the aforementioned shortcomings of concrete have not significantly put the material into question, and it continues to be regarded as a symbol of progress and prosperity, not least due to its importance to the buildings of the post-independence period. In contrast, shame and poverty are associated with vernacular buildings. Our work draws inspiration from both the evolving demands toward the built environments by societies that are moving from self-sustenance to being integrated into the global economy, and the materials, forms, and construction techniques of vernacular architecture. For us, a possible solution for the current crisis lies in the production of an alternative to concrete blocks that respects the call for densification yet becomes conscious of its environmental and social impact.

●8 **Wax Fabric Print with a Concrete House Motif**

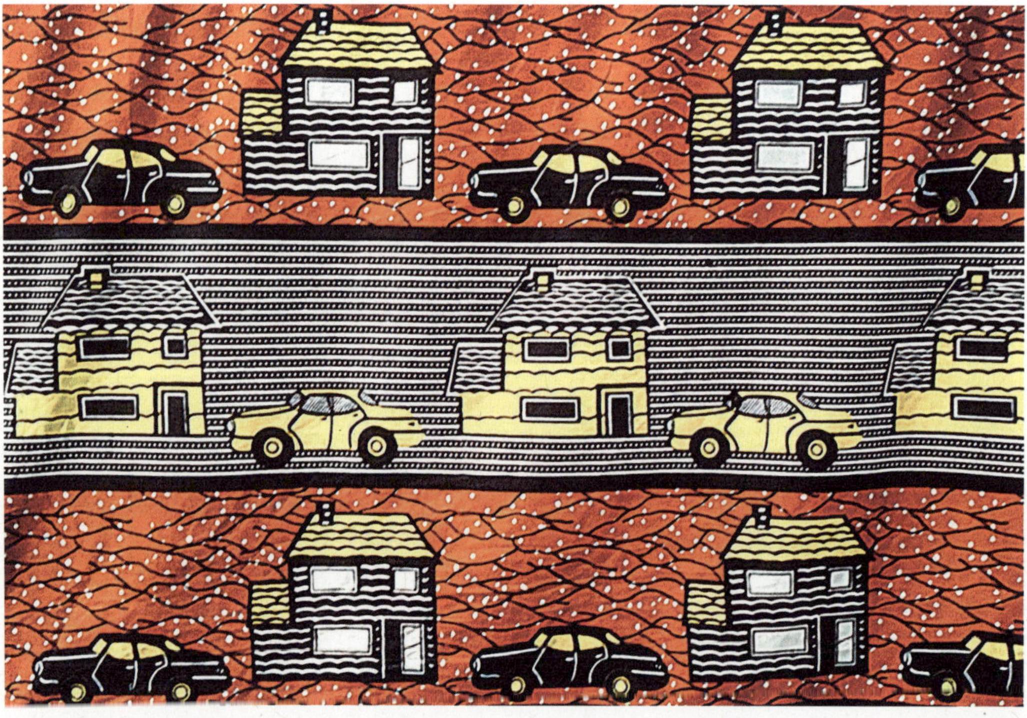

Voices: Acts of Building in Mako

A Conversation between Thierno Dabo and Christian Gaeth

Thierno Dabo and Christian Gaeth are founding members of Studio Suddo Neuve. They have been involved with the collective's projects in different capacities and roles over the years. In the following conversation they examine how the built environment has transformed in Mako, Senegal. As an example, Thierno recalls how he built his first house together with his brother from concrete blocks and compares it to the mud huts his family built when he was a child. The edited transcript is a compilation of a series of conversations.

Thierno Dabo We started constructing this house in 2017, when Studio Suddo Neuve was a mere vision without physical manifestations. My father gave the land to my brother and I to build a new house for our future families.

Christian Gaeth Where is the plot located?

TD Right next to my family's compound. All the surrounding land belongs to my father, we used to work the land here, planting corn and peanuts. But things changed, the neighborhood changed. The farming was scaled back and moved to the fields outside the village and more buildings have been constructed. Also, my family has built some more buildings here. We used to only have two buildings and some huts around the central courtyard of my family's plot. Then my oldest brother built a building for his wife and children outside the compound and when my other brother and I started working in the gold mine, we started building, too. Every month each of us gave 60,000 CFA francs (€91.50) to build the house.

CG How long did it take you to build the house?

TD It was a slow process of around three years. It took us twenty-four months to do the foundations, masonry, and roofing. Then it took us another year to mount windows and doors, finish the surfaces and do installations. But the process was also delayed as we had a family emergency to tend to in the middle of the construction process and had to allocate our building funds to the medical bills. And since me and my brother are both working in the gold mine, we cannot do any of the work ourselves, but must pay workers for it, so it was expensive and tedious to arrange workers without any supervision from our side.

CG What kind of work would you usually do yourself?

TD Well, it starts with simple things such as water. Mixing concrete takes a lot of water and as there was no running water where we were building, we had to get it either from a well or from the river. Since we are not in the village for most of the day, we have to pay Kao Mamadou (the driver) to get water with his tricycle. If the workers don't have enough of it they stop working, yet you pay them for the day of work. One charge of water is ten 20-liter jerricans and he charges us 1,000 CFA francs (€1.53) for it. On a usual day of construction, they go through two charges. So, of our monthly construction budget, we would spend more than 25 percent just on water when we needed it to mix concrete for bricks, mortar, and plaster.

CG That is a lot of money for just water. So, if you are out of the village during the day, who is in charge of the construction and who is working on site?

TD There are different building trades now, but the masons are the managers here. Once we got the land from our father, we invited a mason to the site and discussed with him how many rooms we can fit into one building on the property. Most masons in the town are not from Mako, but learned the trade in the cities and now moved here because a lot of people are building. The masons help with the planning; there are some clear standards that everybody follows here: for example, rooms are between 9 and 12 square meters large. After the planning was done, the mason told us how many bricks we would roughly need, so we hired two brickmakers. They manually mixed the concrete and molded it into a steel form to produce the concrete blocks you see everywhere in Mako now. In the big cities you can buy truckloads of these bricks that are made in factories, but here everybody makes their bricks on site. Once the bricks were made, we called our mason again to execute the construction with a small team of helpers. After they completed all the openings, the welder came to take the measurements of the windows and the doors. The masons also did the plastering once the open elements were installed. We then hired a woodworker for the roofing, then a painter for painting the walls, and a tiler for finishing the floors. However, many people in Mako save costs by leaving out the paint and the tiles.

CG Most concrete houses have corrugated sheet metal, but some also have concrete ceilings. What is the difference between the two construction techniques and why did you decide to build a house with a metal roof?

TD We really wanted to have a concrete ceiling, because then it would be cooler inside, and we could build another story on top once we have money. But concrete ceilings are very expensive as they use a lot of material and need additional equipment for the formwork that is hard to rent in Mako, so we had to go with the sheet metal. In order to make it a little bit cooler though we built the ceiling very high, so that the hot air can rise, and it is not too hot when we are trying to sleep.

CG I remember that when we first met in Mako in 2015, there were very few concrete houses here, now most families have at least one house built with concrete bricks, and you even see multistory construction by the main road. How would you describe the changes of the architecture in Mako?

TD I mean, you can still see the mud huts all over town, but they are becoming less and less. Everybody is building with concrete blocks now; you rarely see people building new huts from earth. Back when I was a child, families used to find a big mango tree and then start building huts around it. Each hut had one room and was only used for sleeping and storing valuables. Then there usually was an additional hut to store food and firewood. These huts are cheap and easy to construct. You can easily build one with your family in one week. And then you just find a neighbor who does the thatch roof for you. But they also don't last very long. The rains are very heavy here during the rainy season and if you don't replaster the walls every two years, the huts will collapse after five or six years. Concrete buildings don't erode and once they are finished and painted you don't have to worry about plastering them. Now that people have money from the work in the gold mine or in restaurants, they mostly build with concrete.

CG You have told me that the mud huts in Mako are an adaptation of the **Fula** typology called *Bukkaru* or *Suddu Hudo* from pastoral times. As the Fula moved their herds throughout the Sahel the architecture needed to be fast to construct and mainly consisted of reed mats and sticks; the disassembled structures were carried by donkeys or other cattle. As the Fula became more sedentary, focusing on agricultural production in addition to herding, the *Bakkaru* was adapted into a concentric mud hut, which uses a similar technique as the *Bukkaru* for its roof structure and simply reinforced the reed mats with earth to build proper walls with a thermal mass. Could you

●9 Vernacular Earth Hut under Construction in Senegal ●10 Unfinished Concrete Structure in Senegal

tell me more about the construction process of the huts nowadays?

TD Building the *Suddos* (Fula name for huts) is very simple, we would mark a circle on the floor and then each family had their own technique to build the walls. Most commonly, people would look for soil with high clay content on their property and then dig it out, mix it with water and plant fiber from wheat and then press it into a wooden form. The brick would then dry for a week in the sun before being used to construct the hut. For the mortar and plaster we would also just use the clay. Some huts now also have concrete plaster to avoid erosion. The roof is traditionally made from bamboo frames and grass mats and is constructed on the ground and then lifted on top of the hut. Alternatively, people would use woven bamboo mats for the wall construction and then compress the earth in between two mats, finishing the construction by plastering the bamboo mats, usually only from the outside. ●9

CG So, would you say that the construction of the huts is also much more spontaneous, as the materials are not procured from traders and no plans need to be made before?

TD Not entirely. With the huts, we had to do the construction during the dry season, because if there is rain before the building is completely dried and protected by the overhanging roof, it will immediately erode. With concrete, people have more flexibility

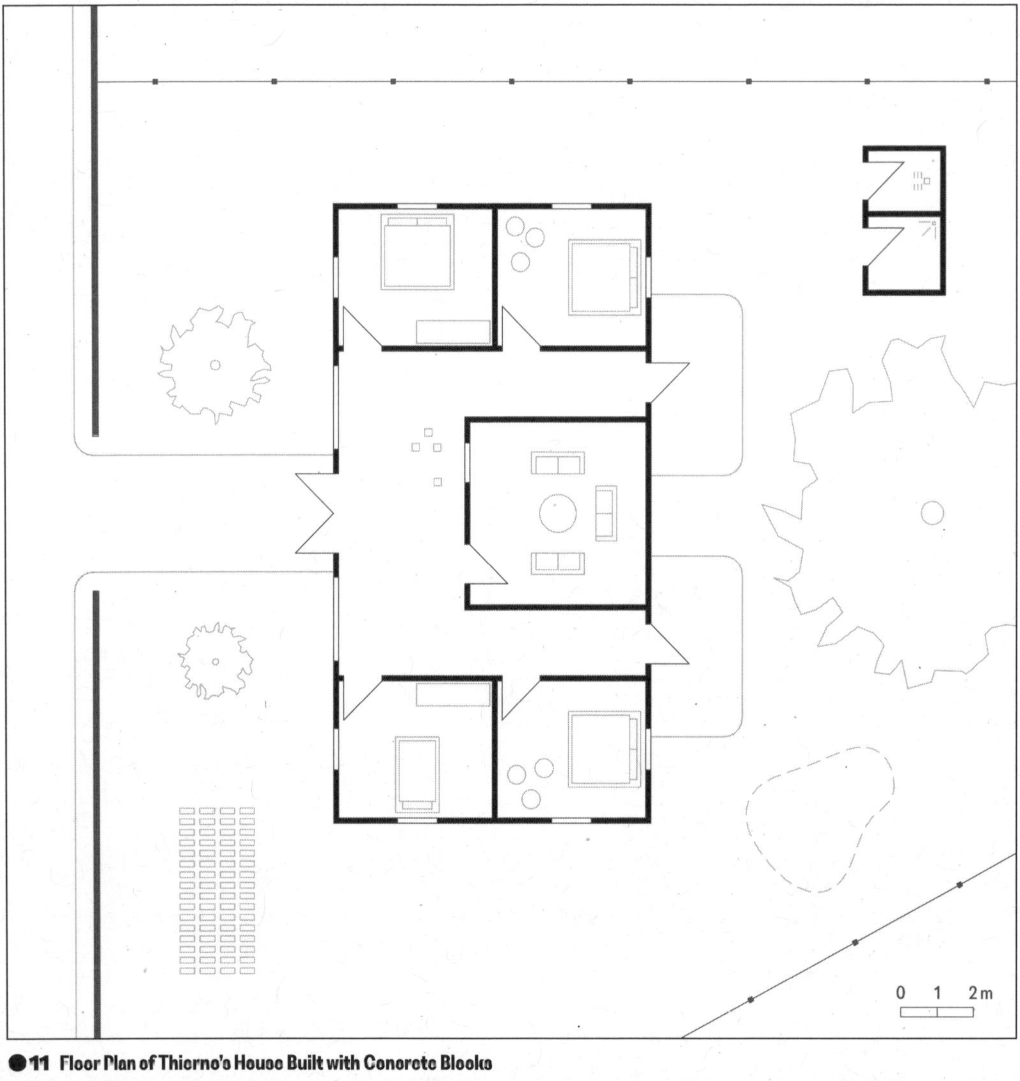

●11 **Floor Plan of Thierno's House Built with Concrete Blocks**

with the construction. Obviously, you do not want to pour a new floor slab in heavy rain, but even during the rainy season many people are building with concrete. ●10

CG I am looking at your concrete house and how it is much bigger than the huts; it has an entrance hall and then two corridors that connect to each side of the building. Each hallway leads to two rooms and at the center of the house you have a salon, a larger communal space. Most houses in Mako only have bedrooms and life happens in the courtyard. Why did you decide to build a salon?

TD We have families in the big cities, and all of them have living rooms, with a TV and some nice furniture. It's where you welcome your guests or where the elder can sit in the shade of the sun. With the solar panels, we also got a TV and can keep it in there and invite the neighborhood to watch it with us. Also, Mako is transforming into a city. Most of the land you see here is taken and people start building everywhere. Especially now with the gold mine, there are many people who have a job, so they have money to start a family and build their own house. All the newer buildings don't have the typical courtyard with the mango tree anymore. Instead, people are building even two or three stories high now. ●11

CG But the courtyards of the compounds do not only function as outside salons; many more activities happen there that cannot happen inside. How did the function of the courtyard change?

TD Our courtyards used to be the center of life for our families. And for many families it still is. We cook, we play, we make tea, and do many other works like cracking peanuts, drying corn, or chopping wood. But you know, less people are farmers with the work in the mines and there is less work to do in the household. Instead of planting, harvesting, drying, and shucking corn, people now buy rice in big bags. People now prefer to cook with charcoal or even gas, so there is no longer a need to chop and store firewood. We used to also have more animals, like sheep and chickens, but if you work it is difficult to take care of them. So, the families that live off wage labor have shifted their work away from the home and toward formal workplaces, so there is less space required for those activities. But the outside space is still essential, and most houses still have a terrace or some garden space.

CG In a sense, I look at your new building and I see how there is still a courtyard at the center as your new living room. Instead of clustering huts around a central outdoor space, your building features rooms around a central living room space. Was this an intentional decision?

TD I have never looked at it that way, but my brother and I were mostly thinking of creating an indoor space for the evenings to hang out with our wives and friends.

CG So, the activities in the courtyard or salon start to evolve more and more around leisure than work?

TD Yes.

CG Earlier you mentioned that you were paying a lot of money for the construction of your building. Why do you think so many people have started to shift from earth huts to concrete buildings? Would you say the concrete houses are better?

TD I am not sure. You know every year when the dry season starts and it starts to get hot, my little brothers fight about who gets to sleep in the huts because they are so much cooler than the concrete house. But it is also so much easier to keep the concrete houses clean, and hence, less work. Replastering the houses also takes a lot of time, with a cinderblock house you don't have to worry if it will stand through the rainy season. So, I'm not sure that concrete is better but for now it is what most people like, because it gives them more stability.

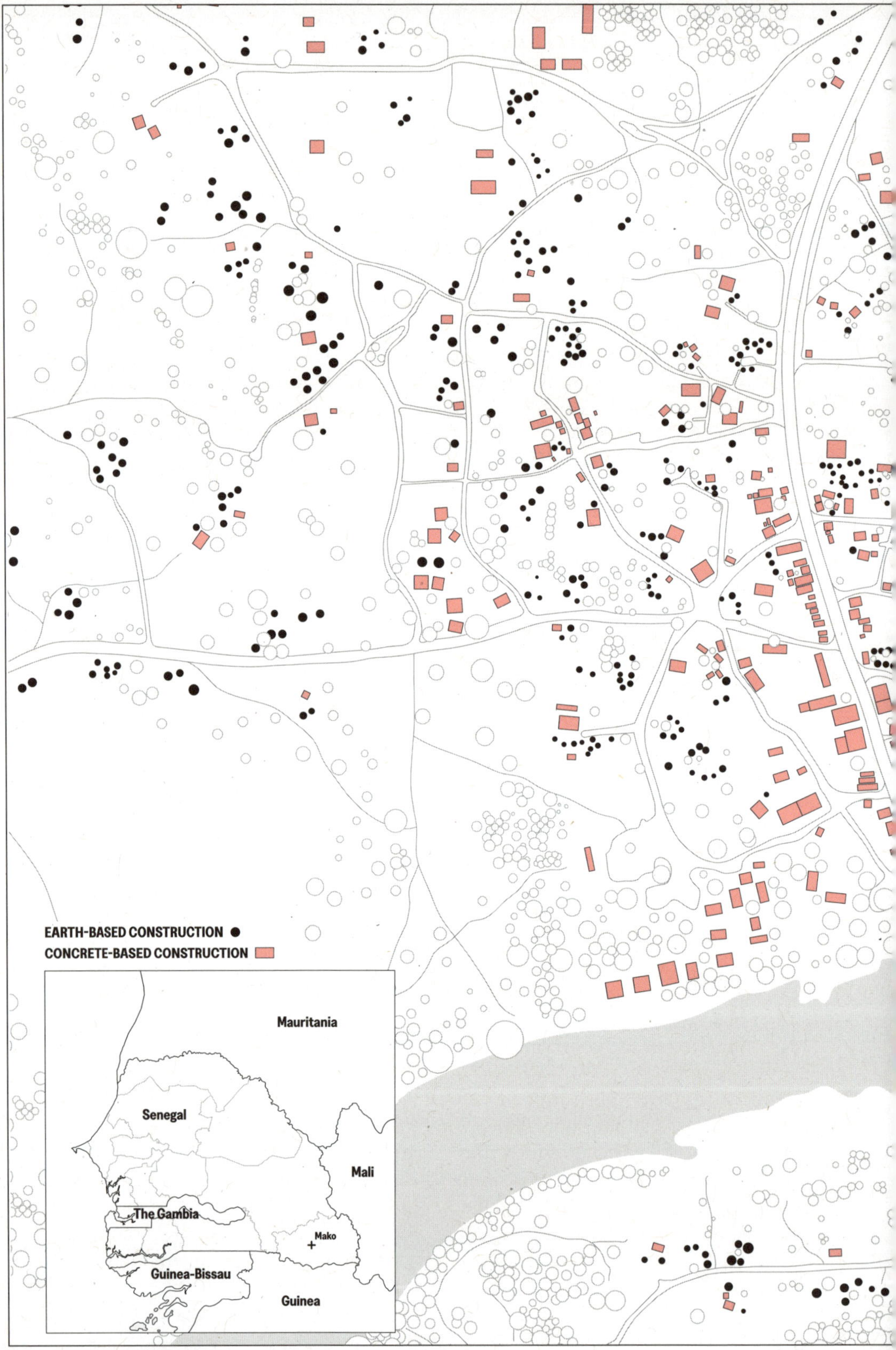
EARTH-BASED CONSTRUCTION
CONCRETE-BASED CONSTRUCTION
Mauritania
Senegal
Mali
The Gambia
Mako
Guinea-Bissau
Guinea

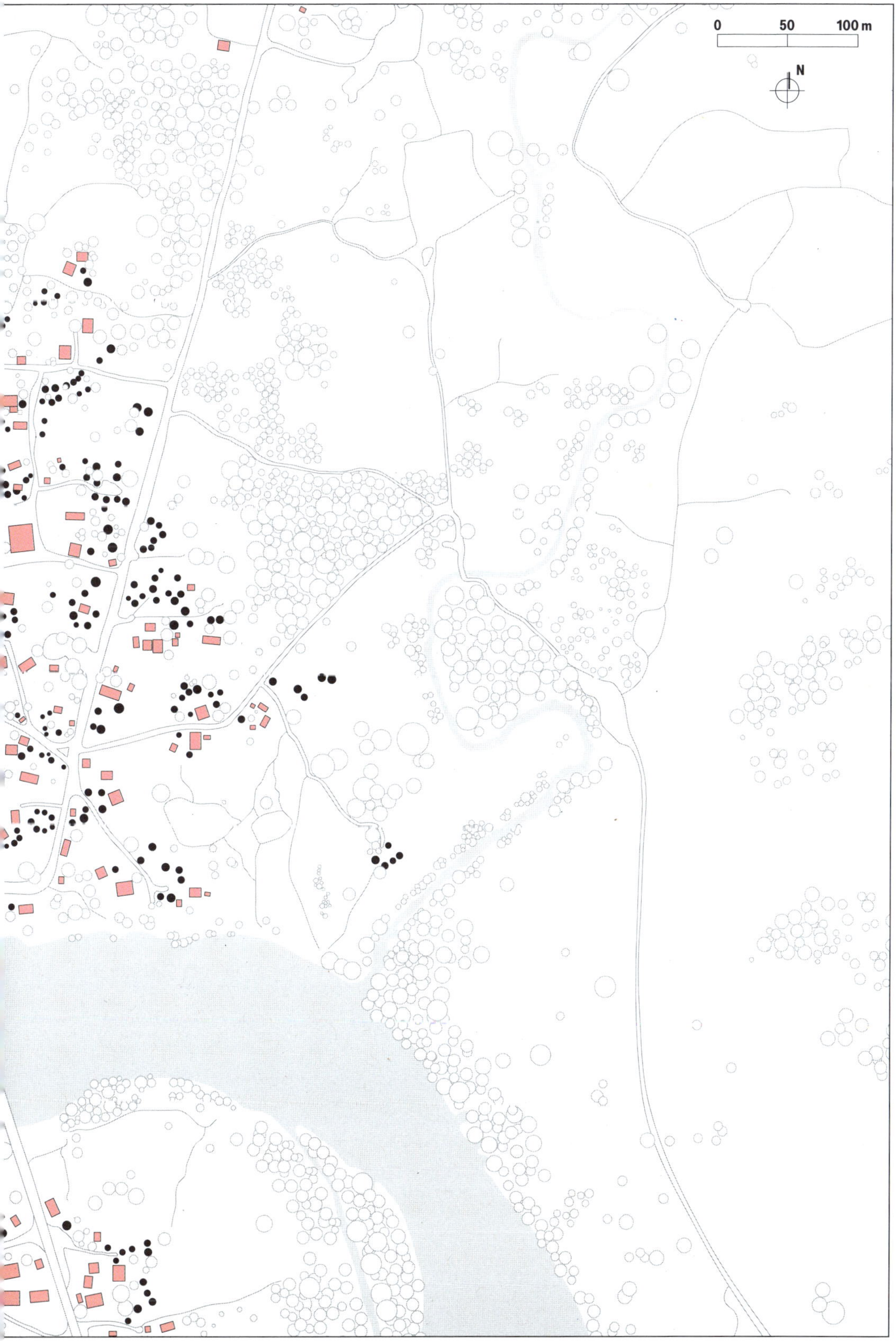

12 Status Quo: Distribution of Earth and Concrete Architecture in Mako, Senegal

Intervention

Gold Rush

The specificities of the material shift from nature-based earth and bamboo to industrial concrete and steel are contextualized in many communities in Senegal. Propelled by substantial influences from the mining and transportation sectors, the village of Mako, situated in the southeastern region of the country, has undergone a notably fast-paced transformation. The work of Studio Suddo Neuve is positioned within the framework of this rapid urbanization phenomenon, and stems from a tripartite approach: an analysis of local urbanization dynamics, an examination of the previously predominant earth-based construction culture, and material investigations to re-entangle contemporary construction with its regional framework.

Mako, with a population of five thousand people, adjoins the Niokolo Koba National Park to the west, and the Gambia River to the east. ●**12** The region is characterized by its fertile red soil of volcanic origin. Heavy rains during the June–October rainy season transform the hills into a thick jungle-like forest, home to rich flora and fauna. During the dry season much of the shrubs and grasses dry out and the plant cover becomes lighter. A two-lane highway running midway through the village connects the region to the country's more populated coast.

30 According to the 2022 Sustainability Report of Resolute, the operating mine, https://www.rml.com.au/wp-content/uploads/2023/05/2547415.pdf, last accessed June 17, 2024.

31 As reported by Mako Exploration Company SA, the mine developer, in their 2015 Environmental and Social Assessment, https://minedocs.com/20/Maco_ESIA_Project-Description_December2015.pdf, last accessed June 17, 2024.

Historically inhabited by small-scale farmers and pastoral communities, the village experienced a turnover when a gold mine started its explorations in 2016 in its immediate vicinity. The mine is expected to produce 740,000 ounces of gold (worth US$202 million) until 2027.[30] This is a volume that amounts to a mere 1.2 cubic meters of gold but requires moving at least 74 million tons of "waste rock" in its extraction.[31] The economic shift from largely self-sufficient farming and crafts to wage labor in the mining sector has significantly impacted the demographics of the community. Migrant workers from the wider region have moved to the community, doubling the population in less than ten years.

Additionally, a 2015 decree by the local government of Kedougou City, the region's capital, prohibiting trucks to stop and park within Kedougou's city limits has had a direct impact on Mako's economy and cityscape. The trucks pass through the region to supply landlocked Mali with imported goods, mostly fuel. As the crossing of the nearby national park can be precarious at night, most drivers used to make a stop in Kedougou City. With the changed policy, however, Mako became the main stopping point for trucks, leading to the development of a service economy of restaurants and mechanics around the main road, allowing women in particular to be economically integrated through food-based small businesses.

The built environment has responded to these changes by shifting its centers of communal life from the river, courtyards, and places of worship toward the highway. The added financial resources are fueling the rapid transformation of Mako to cater to these social developments: private construction projects are providing the localities to process the import and sale of industrial products and the typologies to house and feed migrant workers and truck drivers. Additionally, public infrastructure projects are improving accessibility to services such as education and health care, and developing large-scale technical systems around water and electricity. Accordingly, the importance of private solar power systems and decentralized water extraction from wells and pumps is decreasing.

The highway, the town's center of activities, is lined with small shops and restaurants on both sides. The shops sell food, clothing, basic building materials, and mechanical supplies for bicycles and motorbikes. The restaurants serve dishes by the plate to travelers, teachers, and miners. The buildings on the road are mostly oriented toward the street, constructed of cinder blocks and covered with corrugated sheet metal roofs. Single-story structures remain the most common type, though multistory structures are increasing in number and size.

Mud huts often complement the plots in the courtyard and are used as storage, wet rooms, or animal shelters. Shopkeepers use old oil barrels filled with concrete to prevent trucks from parking directly in front of their shops and restaurants (→ *pp. 34–35* on the distribution of earth and concrete architecture in Mako).

After a decade of ever-faster transformative processes, a critical verdict of Mako's urbanization must be delivered. The introduction of wage labor, capital, and imported building materials has caused a rift between the community and the surrounding natural environment. Based on the false notion that adapting modernity to the local context must align with the materials and production methods of fossil-fuel-dependent societies, the integration of nature-based materials was deemed inconceivable, contributing to the environmental harm inflicted by the construction sector. The resulting urban fabric is an artefact of this disconnect, suffering from an architecture of low performance and short lifespans that struggles to justify its enormous natural and financial costs. ●13

Material Culture

Against this backdrop we sought to develop an architecture that would dissolve the currently mutually exclusive relationship between vernacular architecture and contemporary demands, moving the built environment into a cohesive form. Instead of supporting global universalization through concrete block houses, we want to foster a building culture of regionalism that is as much contemporary and desirable as it is sustainable with regards to regional and ultimately planetary boundaries. Therefore, we designed an intervention that interrogates material and form to understand the potential of incorporating local, low-carbon, and recyclable materials into the transition of architecture toward urban typologies. Mako became our testing ground to re-entangle architecture with its locality and the natural environment.

More broadly, timber construction has been praised as one solution in the global effort to address the climate challenges in the construction sector. With its property of storing carbon, wood, if kept in use long enough, can reduce the carbon dioxide concentration in the atmosphere. However, while wood construction is a viable option in countries with sufficient, suitable, and sustainably managed timber resources, it cannot be applied to every geographical context. In the Sahel, there is not only a large infrastructure gap in the processing of timber into usable construction materials but using wood as the primary construction material would further add pressure to the already strained forests in the

● 13 Construction of a Concrete House in Mako, Senegal

● 14 Townscape of Mako

32 J. Uzu et al., "Timber Business in West Africa: A Review and Outlook," *International Forestry Review* 24, no. 2 (July 2022): 240–56.

region.[32] In our analysis of vernacular architecture in Mako, we found timber to be used sparingly; with some houses using local timber that is manually processed into rough beams for roof constructions, while most houses are using bamboo for these purposes. Most frequently the local hardwood is used for furniture items and not for construction.

Another material to be considered in the context of a decarbonized built environment is earth. Before industrialization and colonization, earth, which was used in the first human settlements as early as ten thousand years ago, was the most widely used building material around the world. Due to its low cost and wide availability, it is in most regions a truly universal building material.

Over the past millennia, many different earth-building methods have developed in West Africa, adapted to the local soils and climatic conditions. However, in the twentieth century, under the impression that fossil fuels would provide an inexhaustible source of energy, earth construction fell out of favor and was not translated to an urban form, thereby displacing a local, abundant, low-cost, and low-carbon resource with concrete, an imported, high-cost and high-carbon industrial composite.

In Mako, the shift away from earth-based construction is as recent as the opening of the gold mine and was driven by two main factors, which continue to pose difficulty for the resumption of earth-based building. Firstly, the demand for multistory buildings requires materials with improved performance capabilities in respect to compressive strength. Secondly, there is a growing desire to minimize building maintenance. Here, the natural erosion of the earth walls during the rainy season compromises their cost effectiveness. ●14

Regardless, earth has significant potential as a high-performance building material in the context of Mako's urbanization and contemporary architecture. The advantages of earth architecture in the climate-specific context of Mako are evident in the superior performance of the vernacular buildings constructed from earth. Due to earth's susceptibility to water, which enables it to store and release moisture, it actively reduces fluctuations in indoor humidity levels. Further, the density of earth materials means they are effective at insulating against heat and sound. Naturally, earth became the focus of our work in Mako.

Internationally, earth's reintroduction into the urban built environment has been pioneered by different architects and organizations. Yet, despite successfully addressing the challenges of multilevel and water-resistant construction, none of the earth-based

●15 Hotel Le Djoloff, CSEB Building in Dakar

33 Gernot Minke, *Building with Earth: Design and Technology of a Sustainable Architecture* (Basel; Boston: Birkhäuser, 2006), 19.

demonstration buildings has had the leverage to have a significant impact on local construction industries. The funding of these endeavors seems intrinsically linked to the deep pockets of prestige projects and not focused on the development of replicable typologies. The scope of our intervention therefore extended beyond the presentation of a demonstration building to the design and establishment of supply chains and capacities to independently execute construction projects. Our goal was to develop a profound understanding of earth as a building material within the specific local context that would allow us to embed it into contemporary paradigms of the building industry and allow it to grow into a self-reproducing industry. The project proposes to intervene in the current habit of choosing global over local and cement over clay. Here, instead of building isolated demonstration buildings that are complicated—or even impossible—to replicate, we are attempting to reintroduce earth as a material to local value chains, inviting local actors to continue and modify the technology. ●15

From Sediment to Block

In the construction context, the term *earth* generally refers to loam-based, non-organic, mineral materials. Loam, the product of the erosion of natural rock, comprises gravel, sand, silt, and clay. The erosion is caused by water, wind, or movement due to thermal contraction and expansion; chemical reactions caused by organic acids, water, or atmospheric gases can have the same effect. The grain-size distribution of the resulting sediments as well as their mineral composition—and hence, their properties—are therefore highly specific to their locality.[33] As a result, different earth-building techniques developed in different areas according to the properties of locally available loam.

Clay, the material with the finest grain, is the natural binder for all the larger particles in loam. Solely activated by water, clay acts similarly to cement in concrete and can produce strong bonds, qualifying earth for load-bearing construction. In contrast to hydraulic binders such as cement and chalk, clay's binding is reversible as it becomes plastic when wet, making it entirely reusable at the end of the life cycle of a building. The water-initiated plasticity of loam enables uncomplicated repair and maintenance of earth-based building parts. However, this susceptibility to water also makes earth a high-maintenance building material, limiting its adoption in societies shaped by industrialization and specialization. ●16

In the past century, earthen building materials have been adapted to address their water sensitivity. Most commonly the earth is fired to irreversibly solidify

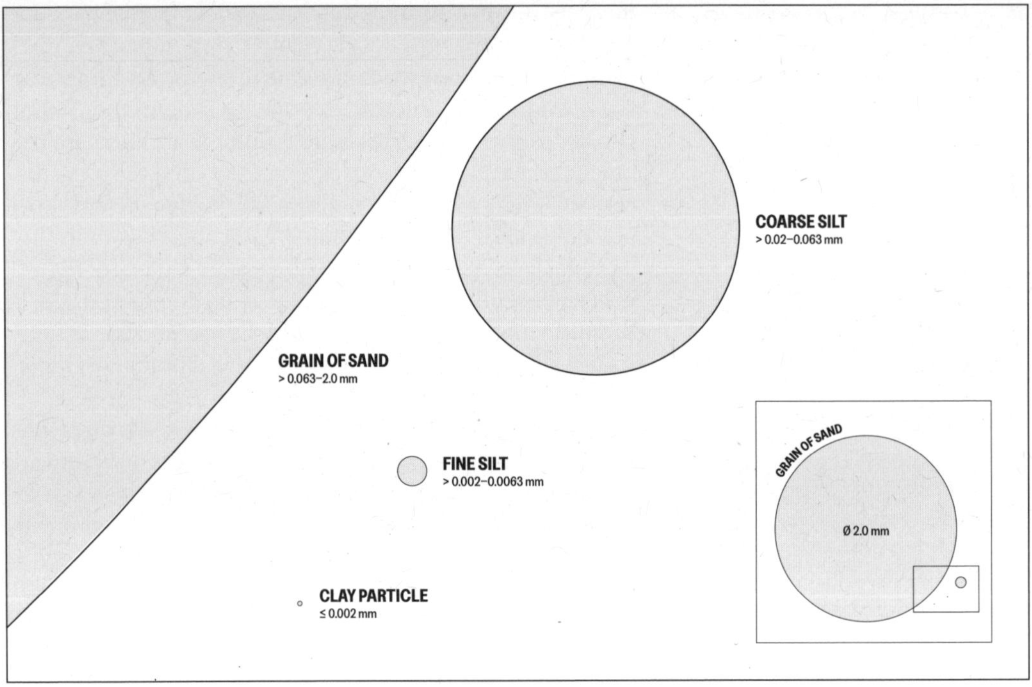

●16 Grain Sizes of Loam/Earth at Scale (Clay, Silt, Sand, and Gravel)

the binding of clay. Further, fired bricks have been tailored to meet the demands of industrialized construction in terms of quality persistence and dimensions and continue therefore to play a crucial role as a construction material. However, the improvement in durability comes with a high energy cost and a great reduction in the reuse potential. Similarly, cement and other hydraulic binders are used to create composites with sedimental aggregates that form irreversible bonds and require significant amounts of primary energy in their production. In the context of decarbonizing the construction industry, unfired and pure earth materials are therefore noteworthy due to their significantly lower energy requirement and their reusability.

The reusability of earth materials becomes of greater significance in light of the global consumption of mineral resources. Sand is being used at an unprecedented rate of 17 kilograms per person per day, with many regions already experiencing scarcity of sand and gravel.[34] Due to the irreversibility of the bonding of sand and gravel with hydraulic binders in the production of concrete, and with clay in case of fired bricks, the mineral resources are torn from the natural rhythms of re- and degeneration for an indefinite period of time.

The irresponsible consumption of sediments is therefore not only causing the destruction of the natural environment through their extraction in open pit mines or from riverbeds, but is also threatening the balance of the natural processes that would secure the regeneration of mineral materials through the natural rock cycle. Earth-based building materials that are relying on clay as their binder can reenter the natural sedimentation process in their initial state without any risk of unintended consequences. Using earth as a primary building material is therefore not only reducing energy consumption and emissions in the production process but is also ensuring less production of anthropogenic matter in the process of demolition.[35] In the conception of the material repertoire for regenerative construction in Mako, earth should therefore play an important role as a substitute for temperature-altered mineral materials. ●17

In Mako, the abandonment of traditional earth construction gave prominence to the masonry trade to execute the concrete-centered urbanization. Earth construction has only sustained a minor role in self-build projects in Senegal in the form of mud huts. Now, new processing techniques must be developed and implemented to make earth compatible with the realities of construction processes and labor specialization without majorly increasing its naturally low ecological footprint. Among the numerous processing possibilities of earth, earth blocks appeared to hold the greatest potential as the material successor of traditional earth architecture and the environmental adaptation of concrete masonry.

Globally, mechanically compressed earth blocks have been discussed as an economically and ecologically efficient alternative to fired bricks and concrete blocks. The compaction of earth increases its compressive strength and resistance to water, rendering the material adequate for load bearing, multistory construction. The mechanical pressing of earth into bricks has been explored since the late eighteenth century. Its origins can be traced to the works of François Cointeraux, who, during the French Revolution, sought ways to industrialize earth.[36] For this purpose, he developed a mechanical press called La Crésise, which rationalized the traditional handling of clay and attempted to interpret the building material in the spirit of the new era.[37] While Cointeraux's pioneering work involved compacting earth through a falling weight into a formwork, an adapted system where loam is compressed by a movable plate in a steel chamber was developed in the twentieth century and applied in different variations by various manufacturers. The resulting **compressed earth blocks** (CEBs) can be produced under controlled conditions and therefore show a high degree of quality consistency, which qualifies them for load-bearing applications. In view of the current construction activity, it is noteworthy that the complexity of almost all building efforts lies within the structural capabilities of these earth blocks.

34 United Nations Environment Programme, *Sand and Sustainability: Finding New Solutions for Environmental Governance of Global Sand Resources* (Geneva, 2019).

35 In 2018, construction and demolition waste (CDW) was estimated to total about 1.68 kilograms per person per day globally. Emina Kristina Petrović and Caroline Ann Thomas, "Global Patterns in Construction and Demolition Waste (C&DW) Research: A Bibliometric Analysis Using VOSviewer," *Sustainability* 16, no. 4 (January 2024): 1561.

36 Sigismund Friedrich Hermbstaedt, *Bulletin des Neuesten und Wissenswürdigsten aus der Naturwissenschaft, so wie den Künsten, Manufakturen, technischen Gewerben der Landwirtschaft und der bürgerlichen Haushaltung* (Amelang, 1813); Louis Bouchard-Huzard, *Traité des constructions rurales et de leur disposition* (Paris: Mme. V. Bouchard-huzard, 1869), http://archive.org/details/traitedesconstru02bouc, last accessed September 23, 2024.

37 Jean Dethier, Heinrich Klotz, and Karl Heinz Striedter, *Lehmarchitektur: Die Zukunft einer vergessenen Bautradition* (Munich: Prestel Verlag, 1982), 13.

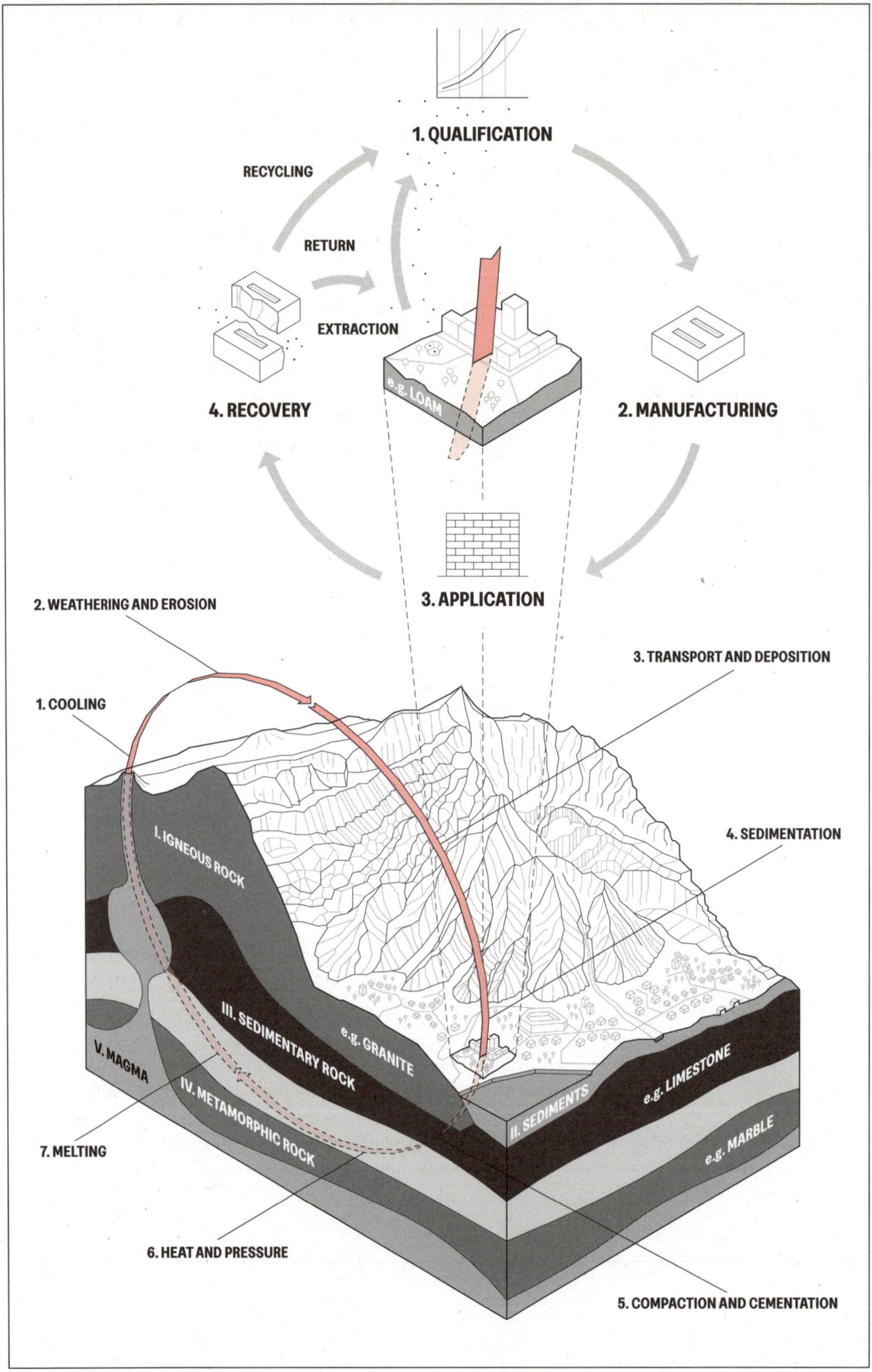

●17 Earth-Based Construction and the Natural Rock Cycle

In the development of CEBs for Mako, we considered many existing handbooks and publications for a basic understanding of the required processes and techniques.[38] Additionally, we orientated the quality standards and testing procedures of the blocks on existing building codes.[39] Several indicators for producing CEBs were distilled from a wide range of academic sources and technical standards and applied to the local circumstances. While the Manual chapter *(→ pp. 59–95)* of this publication details the process of setting up an earth-block production site and using earth blocks in construction, the following pages summarize our process of developing CEBs and supplement theoretical knowledge on earth-based building materials with the learnings from our experiments in a non-laboratory environment.

Earth Block Experiments

Following the recommendations of the reviewed sources, two parameters proved to be crucial to produce high performing blocks, and were the primary concern of our initial experimentations. Firstly, the dry density of earth-based materials is directly correlated to the compressive strength.[40] Higher levels of compaction result in high levels of compressive strength, which is crucial when the blocks are intended to be used in load-bearing construction. This force can only be achieved by using a machine that multiplies the force input of humans or an engine through levers. Additionally, lower water content during the pressing results in a higher dry density. The process-water content must hence be optimized to allow for sufficient plasticity during the manufacturing process and maximum density when the blocks have dried. Secondly, knowing the grain-size distribution of the raw material is crucial to produce high-performing blocks. The interplay of the different grain-size fractions affects the cohesiveness of the block, where large and small particles are equally important to form a stable composite through the compression. Furthermore, the granular structure and mineral composition also determine the susceptibility to moisture-related swelling and shrinkage and are therefore key indicators for the suitability of a primary material. The grain-size distribution of soil is determined through a combined sieve and sedimentation analysis. This process involves separating individual grain fractions of sand and gravel through sieving, while the composition of the fine fraction (clay and silt) is determined through a sedimentation procedure. To understand which soil composition is most suitable for the pressing of earth blocks, various international research projects concerning the optimal grain-size distribution were compared.

38 Some of the most comprehensive guides are: Vincent Rigassi and CRATerre-EAG, *Compressed Earth Blocks: Volume 1. Manual of Production* (Braunschweig: Vieweg, 1995); Sid Boubekeur et al., *Compressed Earth Blocks: Testing Procedures* (Brussels: CDE, 2000), https://craterre.hypotheses.org/4003, last accessed September 23, 2024; E.A. Adam and A.R.A. Agib, *Compressed Stabilised Earth Block Manufacture in Sudan* (Paris: UNESCO, July 2001), https://unesdoc.unesco.org/ark:/48223/pf0000128236, last accessed September 23, 2024.

39 Among many, we found the German and the Indian Standards to be most comprehensive and applicable: Deutsches Institut für Normung, ed., DIN 18945:2018-12, *Earth Blocks Requirements, Test and Labelling* (Berlin: Beuth Verlag 2018), https://www.din.de/de/wdc-beuth%3Adin21%3A296262224, last accessed March 31, 2023; Bureau of Indian Standards, *IS 1725: 2023: Stabilized Soil Blocks Used In General Building Construction Specification* (New Delhi, March 2023), http://archive.org/details/gov.in.is.1725.2023, last accessed September 23, 2024.

40 The link between dry density, compaction, and compressive strength has been outlined in: Simon Guihéneuf, Damien Rangeard, and Arnaud Perrot, “Cast, Compaction, Vibro-Compaction or Extrusion: Processing Methods for Optimizing the Mechanical Strength of Raw Earth-Based Materials,” *Academic Journal of Civil Engeneering* 37, no. 2, special issue: 3rd International Conference on Bio-Based Building Materials, Belfast, 2019 (2019): 156–63.

However, other researchers have shown that the correlation of compaction and compressive strength is highly dependent on the specific mineral composition of the loam, see: Minke, *Building with Earth*, 44.

The reviewed sources show clear overlaps in their suggestions for grain-size distributions and indicate that a loamy soil (approximately 10–25 percent mass fraction of clay) with a high content of sand (approximately 55–75 percent mass fraction of sand) serves as an ideal raw material. Silt and gravel are only required in minimal quantities in all references. While the granular structure serves as an indicator for the suitability of a soil as a raw material to produce earth-based building materials, the presence of sufficient amounts of clay particles determined by a sieve and sedimentation analysis can be deceiving. On the one hand there are other minerals with particle sizes equal to those of clay minerals; on the other hand, clay particles can have different properties depending on their mineralogy.[41] This introduces a degree of uncertainty into the interpretation of sieve and sedimentation analyses. Hence, additional tests need to be conducted to avoid misconceptions. In most cases those further tests are easier to perform on block prototypes than on the unprocessed material, especially in the absence of the necessary laboratory equipment.

While a wide variety of different clay soils were available in the immediate vicinity of Mako, a suitable mechanical press was impossible to find in the region. Turning to the internet, we discovered open-source plans for a press that was developed by Raúl Ramírez in 1956 and is known as the Cinva Ram press.[42] It can be produced from welded steel plates. In cooperation with a welder, we built a press according to the plans. However, due to a lack of precision tools, the fabricated press was not usable for seamless production cycles, and we were under the impression that the forces exerted through a single lever translation and by a single human was insufficient to produce blocks suitable for multistory construction. In most cases it is advisable to purchase a block press from an established machine producer as high precision tools and a solid understanding of mechanical engineering is required to produce an efficient block press. As it was our intention to ensure replicability and economic efficiency with our work on CEBs, we purchased an Auram 3000, a manual press with more mechanization and compressive force than the Cinva Ram, which allowed for a higher quality and quantity of production.

With a working press, we set out to find a suitable raw material in Mako to produce earth blocks. Loamy soils around the community have been used in the construction of vernacular architecture for centuries and could be easily sourced from existing borrow pits. The advantage of using soil from these pits was its access to the layers beneath topsoil, thus avoiding the additional removal of fertile soil and guaranteeing organic

41 See samples of the effect of mineralogy on CEB performance: Lavie A. Mango-Itulamya et al., "Evaluation of Belgian Clays for Manufacturing Compressed Earth Blocks," *Geologica Belgica* 22, no. 3–4 (December 15, 2019): 139–48; Japhet Taypondou Darman et al., "Evaluation of Lateritic Soils of Mbé for Use as Compressed Earth Bricks (CEB)," *Heliyon* 8, no. 8 (August 2022).

42 B. V. Venkatarama Reddy, *Compressed Earth Block and Rammed Earth Structures*, Springer Transactions in Civil and Environmental Engineering Ser (Singapore: Springer Singapore Pte. Limited, 2022), 120–22.

free matter. The loamy soils in Mako are mostly laterites, a term which refers to the formation process of the minerals through tropical weathering. Preliminary tests showed that the materials exhibit different characteristics and configuration of granular structure, but generally lacked medium-coarse sand grains, which causes a high degree of drying shrinkage in earth blocks due to the relatively higher clay content. The degree of shrinkage is determined by observing the dimensional change of an earth block throughout the drying process, and if high, indicates the risk of potential crack formation, which reduces the brick's performance. In climates with rainy and dry seasons, the drying shrinkage should be minimized to reduce the risk of cracking between seasons.[43] The swell-shrink characteristics of earth can be controlled by mixing different soils to control the type and relative quantity of clay, silt, sand, and gravel.[44] With the addition of medium-coarse sand to the laterite soil, we reduced the relative clay content and were able to produce earth blocks with high levels of compressive strength, sharp edges, and low abrasion. ●18

The next challenge was solving for water: the blocks we developed were still very susceptible to moisture, a struggle for building in a climate with a heavy rainy season. As the developed material was supposed to be competing with hollow concrete blocks, which are completely water resistant and do not require any maintenance, we also experimented with stabilizing the earth blocks with Portland cement. Most of our references of earth-masonry architecture utilized **compressed stabilized earth blocks** (CSEB) to avoid the additional maintenance of replastering the façades regularly. Alternatively, an additional façade could be added to the building as a rain protection. However, especially

43 Maximilian Brinkmann and Philipp Wiehle, "Correlation between Relative Humidity and the Strength and Deformation Characteristics of Unstabilised Earth Masonry," *Construction and Building Materials* 366 (February 2023).

44 Reddy, *Compressed Earth Block and Rammed Earth Structures*, 429.

●18 Grain-Size Distribution: Mako Soil and Researched References ***(→ p. 134)***

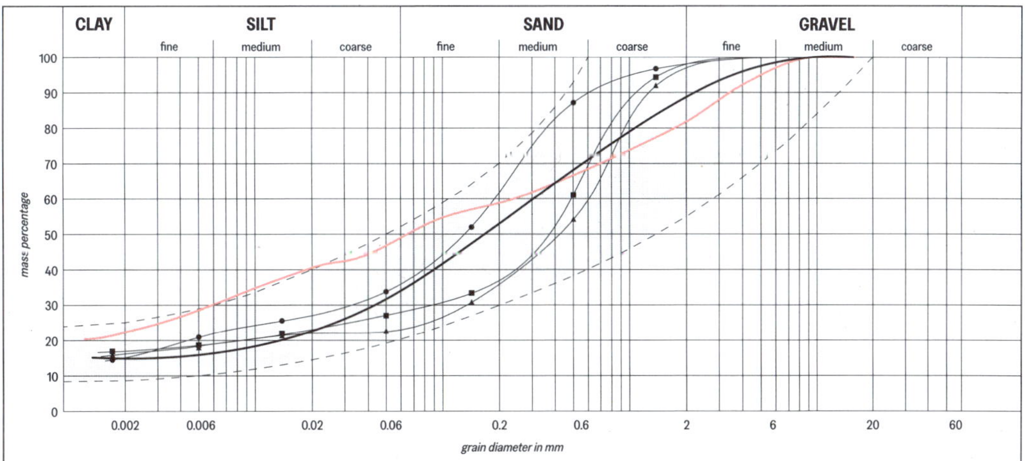

code	(pink line)	(bold line)	(line with dot)	(line with square)	(line with triangle)	(dashed line)
reference	Mako, natural soil	Mako, optimized soil	acc. Minke, 2006 [a]	acc. Boubekeur et al., 2000 [b]	acc. Reddy, 2022 [c]	acc. Rigassi, 1995 [d]
clay content	22%	15%	15%	17%	16%	9–26%

in climates where no additional insulation is needed, the added façade constitutes an additional cost and therefore rendered CSEBs, which acquire water resistance through the stabilization, more cost effective than their unstabilized counterparts. Furthermore, the water resistance of CSEBs is an advantage not only because of the durability of the finished building, but also because a water-resistant material is easier to store and to work with during construction.

However, despite their cost effectiveness and ease of use, CSEBs have significant disadvantages to blocks that are produced without any hydraulic binders.[45] Hydraulic binders, such as cement, render the binding forces of clay ineffective, as the binders' particles work by encasing clay particles to restrict swelling and shrinkage. The result is the destruction of the clay matrix, thereby nullifying the binding force of the clay and its ability to absorb moisture and regulate room climates. Furthermore, the use of cement significantly increases the adverse environmental impact of the blocks and reduces their potential for reuse, as the binding capabilities of the clay are permanently reduced by the stabilizers.

It is important to note how CEBs and CSEBs differ in their respective production processes. While both require a similar grain-size distribution and therefore have to go through the same process of crushing and sieving, CEBs require a more careful preparation of the mix to activate the binding force of the clay minerals. Firstly, it is important to uniformly moisten the earth to a state where it becomes plastic. The plasticity is based on the plate-like geometry of clay minerals. Water surrounds the plates with a thin film, allowing them to slide over each other. Since only simple static pressure is applied during the subsequent pressing and there are no dynamic forces to further mix the soil, thorough preparation of the soil is necessary to achieve maximum binding. After mixing, the loam must rest in the moistened state for twenty-four to forty-eight hours. This process, known as **slaking**, aims to further mobilize the clay platelets activated by the water. Our research has shown significant improvements in compressive strength for earth blocks produced from slaked earth.[46] The adding of fast-curing cement to CSEBs means there is no slaking in their production; instead, the mixture must be immediately processed after adding water. Once both materials are ready—CEBs after mixing and slaking and CSEBs after only mixing—the procedure for pressing and curing the blocks is similar for both.

Living Lab

In order to better understand the performance of CEBs, CSEBs, and hollow concrete blocks in

45 Henri Van Damme and Hugo Houben, "Earth Concrete. Stabilization Revisited," *Cement and Concrete Research*, Report of UNEP Working Group on Low-CO2 Eco-Efficient Cement-Based Materials, 114 (December 1, 2018): 90–102.

46 These findings are supported by Minke, *Building with Earth*, 40–45.

the context of architecture in Mako, Studio Suddo Neuve conducted a **living lab**. Building a number of wall fragments helped us to understand the differences in the production of the blocks and their relative environmental and economic cost effectiveness. The process also allowed us to experiment with additional building components to complement the weaknesses of the earth architecture. As part of the living lab, we produced CEBs and two types of CSEBs, one stabilized with a 3-mass percent cement component and the other with 6 percent. While the block stabilized with 6-percent cement adhered to the general recommendations of experts, the selection of a 3-percent mix aimed to explore the balance between cost (economically and environmentally) and quality. As a control, we also produced the commonly used concrete blocks and built a conventional wall as part of the series. The goal of the living lab is to monitor the performance of the different blocks throughout the different seasons and, over the course of multiple years, to understand patterns of erosion, cracking, and durability. Non-stabilized blocks in particular should be evaluated under these circumstances before being employed in multistory constructions. ●19

After producing the different types of blocks, they were used to build five wall fragments. For this purpose, a series of mortars were developed in parallel to match the cement ratios of the respective blocks. The mortars were based on the same laterite-and-sand mixture as the blocks but sieved to a finer grain to prevent the wedging of gravel in mortar joints. During the construction of the walls, it was evident that there was a difference between the sensitivity of CSEBs and CEBs, especially as the masons were used to laying the much sturdier hollow concrete blocks. Nevertheless, it was equally possible to build a load-bearing wall with the unstabilized blocks *(→ pp. 73–76)*. The construction of the five walls also allowed us to train masons on the use of CSEBs and CEBs, and subsequent projects have been able to benefit from this.

In addition to the different kinds of mixtures, the walls are equipped with different forms of rain protection to reduce the effect of water on the walls. One wall, constructed with pure CEBs, is equipped with an additional bio-based façade made from bamboo to prevent erosion. Since its completion, the surfaces of the walls are regularly examined by our team and their performance documented. That evidence is then used to inform further decisions for the employment of the different blocks and to explain the difference to visitors and clients. ●20

●19 Living Lab: Fragments of CEB, CSEB and Concrete Block Walls

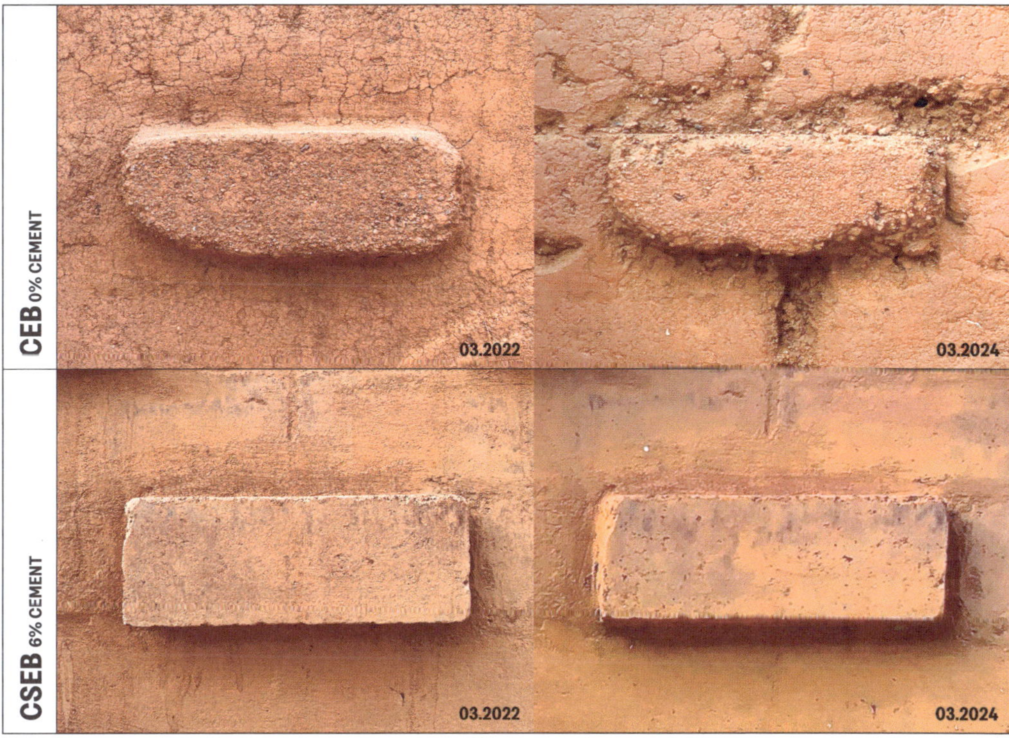

●20 Close-Ups of Living Lab Wall Surfaces over Time

Pricing

Our living lab helped us to understand if we could offer earth blocks at a competitive price point. We documented the production costs of the different block types and were able to compare them throughout the construction process. CSEBs and CEBs are produced with the same means of production, with the only difference of cement. With a team of eleven workers, we were able to produce 800 blocks on a regular working day. By comparison, three brick makers can produce 200 hollow concrete blocks in the same amount of time. Comparing the manufacturing costs (labor and material) for one cubic meter of hollow concrete blocks, one cubic meter of CSEBs, and one cubic meter of CEBs reveals the economic potential of the latter. While 23,250 CFA francs (approximately €36 per cubic meter) is required for concrete blocks, only 8,900 CFA francs (approximately €14) is required to produce the same amount of CSEBs, and 4,900 CFA francs (approximately €7.50) for the equal number of CEBs. However, the clear price advantage of the CSEBs and CEBs needs to be corrected somewhat; a smaller total volume of cinder blocks is required to produce a square meter of wall due to a smaller wall depth (15 centimeters compared to 24 centimeters). On one hand, the narrower brick translates into a lower material requirement, and hence lower construction costs; on the other hand, it means a lower thermal mass and hence less agreeable interior temperatures.

47 Selim Karkour et al., "Status of Life Cycle Assessment (LCA) in Africa." *Environments* 8 (February 5, 2021): 10.

48 Contemporary research on the environmental impact of building in West Africa has also resorted to European LCA data bases. Cf. Lokko et al., "Comparing."

49 A regular, single-story two-bedroom house in Mako requires approximately fifteen cubic meters of masonry blocks.

Apart from the total cost, it is worth considering what those costs of producing the different blocks comprise. Most of the expense of concrete-block production is in the purchasing its constituent materials—sand (62 percent) and cement (15 percent)—both of which are subject to the dominant structures of global infrastructural injustice. For the CSEBs, however, the expenditures are increasingly attributable to labor (30 percent) and earth (40 percent). Since the latter is not a processed good, it must be noted that the costs are comprised of digging, transportation, and unloading, and thus could be regarded as labor costs too. CEBs are even better performers, as none of the financial resources are used for imported building materials. Further technical arguments—for example, CSEB and CEB masonry does not have to be treated any further, hence, saving costs for paint or tiles—stand to their cost advantage (→ *p. 105* for a detailed analysis of auxiliary costs to concrete block, CSEB and CEB construction). The material shift from concrete blocks to CSEBs and/or CEBs can thus be understood as an opportunity to escape the colonial constraints of global capitalism and instead to strengthen local value creation by shifting the allocated resources toward local labor cost. ●21

Comparative Life Cycle Assessment

The significant reduction in cement is thereby directly reducing the environmental footprint of the proposed masonry units. As the global building industry is forced to convert its chronic standards of exploitation and depletion toward circularity and sustainability, CSEBs and CEBs exemplify this transformation by economizing finite and energy intensive mineral resources. The economization of cement is strongly reducing the carbon dioxide emissions of the masonry, while the reduction of sand and gravel is limiting the expansion of extraction sites into ecosystems. To quantify the environmental impact, a **life cycle assessment** (LCA) of the different masonry blocks was conducted. The focus of the LCA lays on the global warming potential (GWP), a parameter that determines the carbon dioxide equivalent of the greenhouse gas emissions emitted during the production of the materials. In this chapter the LCA focuses on the masonry unit, without taking into account the respective construction systems that differ between concrete blocks, CSEBs and CEBs. Reliable and comprehensive LCA data for the West African context is unfortunately not available.[47] Therefore, this analysis uses the German database Ökobaudat to determine the GWP of the different raw materials used in the block production.[48] The conducted LCA analysis includes the extraction of the raw materials, their transportation to

		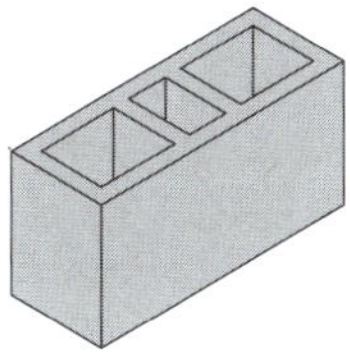	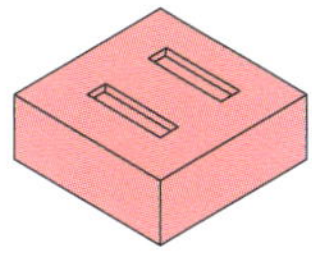	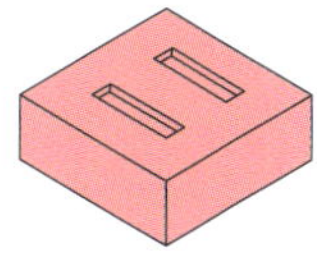
MASONRY TYPE		**CONCRETE BLOCK**	**CSEB**	**CEB**
Dimensions		40 × 15 × 20 cm	24 × 24 × 9 cm	24 × 24 × 9 cm
		MATERIAL COMPOSITION		
Earth		-	64%	67%
Sand		80%	30%	33%
Cement		20%	6%	-
		FINANCIAL COSTS		
CFA Francs / m^3		23,500	8,900	4,900
€ / m^3		35.55	13.57	7.47
Reduction Potential		-	62%	79%
		COST DISTRIBUTION		
Earth		-	40%	42%
Sand		62%	20%	21%
Cement		15%	3%	-
Labor		18%	30%	30%
Tool wear		5%	7%	7%
		ENVIRONMENTAL COSTS		
GWP in kg CO_2-eq. / m^3		515.0	160.8	7.7
Reduction Potential		-	69%	99%
	GWP in kg CO_2-eq. / m^3	**ENVIRONMENTAL COST DISTRIBUTION**		
Earth[a]	9.62	-	4%	83%
Sand[b]	3.85	1%	1%	17%
Cement[c]	2559.38	99%	95%	-

●21 Material Costs and Environmental Impacts of Concrete Block, CSEB and CEB Manufacturing ***(→ p. 134)***

the manufacturing site, and the manufacturing of the blocks (commonly referred to as phases A1-3). The following chapters further complicate this analysis by expanding the calculations to typical housing typologies *(→ pp. 103–105)*.

With a 160.8-kilogram carbon dioxide equivalent per cubic meter, CSEBs exhibits a 69 percent lower GWP than concrete blocks. CEBs further reduce this number to only 7.7 kilograms carbon dioxide equivalent per cubic meter, thereby reducing production-related emissions by more than 99 percent.[49]

CSEBs ... for Now

From an economic and an environmental point of view the CEBs and CSEBs are clearly outcompeting their concrete counterparts. The minimization of imported goods and the focus on simple and constantly available materials and techniques further underpin this flexibility. Additionally, from a social perspective, the local block production creates the opportunity to

SENEGAL (NATIONAL)
KEDOUGOU (REGIONAL)
6% OF TOTAL MATERIAL (BY VOLUME)
MAKO (LOCAL)
MANUFACTURING SITE

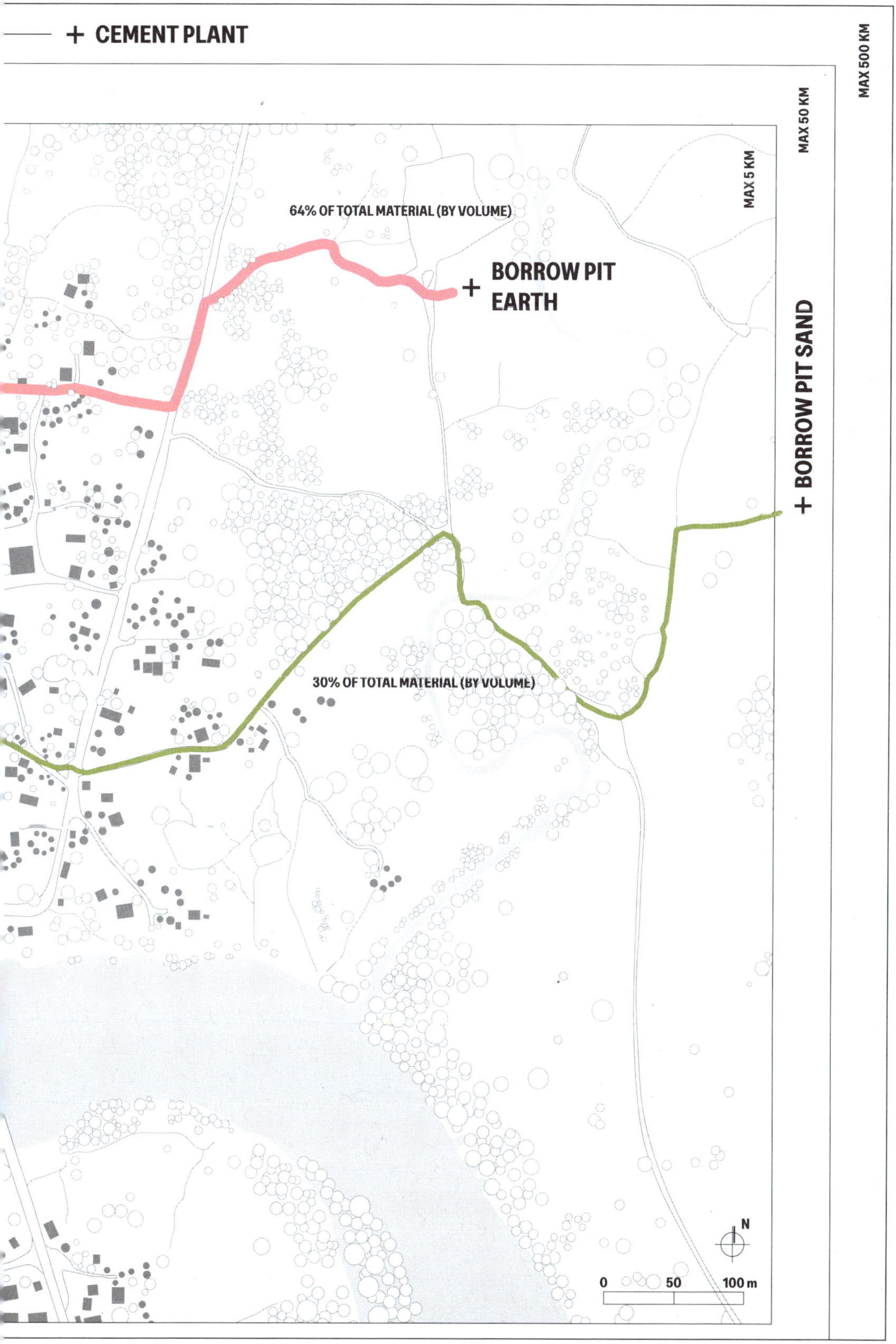

●22 **Material Sourcing: Transport Routes of Earth Block Materials**

keep economic funds within the community. Here, the labor-intensive production of CSEBs and CEBs from local soils stands in contrast to the loss of local funds to large corporations in the global steel and cement industries. Furthermore, they fit into the tradition of a building culture in accordance with availability. They can easily be integrated into the segmented building process and do not require methodological changes to the current habits of construction.

Despite the environmental and building advantages of the CEBs, we decided to move forward with the construction of CSEB buildings in our first demonstration projects. This is largely due to their improved handling on the construction site and their cost advantage when considering that CEBs require either heavy maintenance or an additional building component to waterproof the façade and protect the blocks. This is especially crucial during the construction phase: since funds are allocated to constructions as they are available, the processes can be lengthy and span over multiple rainy seasons. Employing CEBs would require a constant weather protection of the blocks not only once applied in the building but even during the construction process. Currently, it seems difficult to enter the market with a product with these caveats. Furthermore, the CSEBs have an improved compressive strength, which suggests that CSEB multistory constructions are safer.

We will continue to improve the characteristics of the CEBs and monitor our test objects to employ them in construction projects in the future. Another application that we aim to explore is the hybrid construction of CSEBs and CEBs. In this approach, load-bearing exterior walls as well as interior walls of wet areas can be constructed using CSEBs, while simple interior walls, both load-bearing and non-load-bearing, can be made from CEBs *(→ p. 124)*.

Consolidated within the medium of simple earth blocks—unfired, compressed, partially stabilized—our efforts to explore an urbanization without depletion yielded a practical tool for Mako but also a conceptual framework for the local specification of architectures within planetary boundaries. ●22

Manual

The following pages contain the most important information on working with earth blocks. As a manual, these pages are designed to be taken to project meetings and production and construction sites. This chapter, as well as other manuals in this series, are available online in open access format. Scan the QR code to access and share.

Hands On!

After numerous cycles of manufacturing compressed stabilized earth blocks (CSEBs) and evaluating their application and performance in a wide range of architectural constructions, we have distilled our experience into key takeaways. On site, we use these takeaways as guidelines. With this manual, we hope to inspire and empower like-minded initiatives, make the case for practical solutions in the ever-more-urgent debate on architecture and climate change, and increase the acceptance of earth-based materials as an important pillar of regenerative construction. The manual is designed to span the whole life cycle of earth blocks and across material, building and urban scale, to enable the production of not only CSEBs but also CSEB architecture. The manual begins with the identification and sourcing of suitable earth (I). Following an outline of the basic requirements for an effective block manufacturing site, the manual then looks at the optimization and processing of earth for the pressing of CSEBs and enumerates the steps involved in their manufacturing, stacking, and curing (II). In a third step different protocols to assess the quality of earth blocks are explored (III), before the fourth section introduces architectural details that illustrate the use of CSEBs in walls, floor slabs, and roofs as well as their interfaces with other building materials and components (IV). A comment on the maintenance and deconstruction of CSEB construction completes the manual (V).

While this manual is not comprehensive, it reflects the most essential components of building that are close to universal across building cultures. When confronted with obstacles, such as refining construction details, we embraced the principle of "knowing enough to proceed," rather than perfecting details in theory; from our experience, maintaining momentum is crucial, and applying our existing knowledge practically has provided valuable feedback for future improvements and innovations. During particularly challenging situations, we have attempted to evaluate a range of potential solutions through iterative prototyping, both with model and full-scale demonstrations, before making decisions about application.

I Sourcing Raw Materials

Being inherently diverse, soil presents a myriad of compositions and characteristics. Different clay minerals impart distinctive characteristics, requiring an adapted approach for each project. Additionally, the regionally specific climates impose varying stresses and opportunities for earth-based products.

Identifying Raw Materials

Factors such as heavy rainfall and extreme temperature fluctuations pose significant challenges to earth constructions. Prescribing a universally perfect source material remains unattainable. Rather, developing location-specific approaches toward building with earth will help address challenges and meet requirements.

Due to earth's presence in almost all building cultures of the past, building with CSEBs entails a process of revitalizing local soils rather than discovering them. When searching for suitable earth, we advise practitioners to investigate the construction history of the location. Often, this research can lead to the rediscovery of formerly sourced materials and provide insights into the quantities and qualities of local earth as well as traditional mixing and application techniques. **●23**

All earth consists of varying fractions of gravel, sand, silt, clay minerals and, depending on the case, decomposed organic matter and additional minerals. It lies in the distribution of their mass fractions to determine whether the available earth is suitable for CSEBs *(→ pp. 47–50)*. Numerous comprehensive guides for earth analysis in the context of earth building materials are readily accessible. For instance, Vincent Rigassi's publication *Compressed Earth Blocks: Manual of Production* (1985) offers robust methodologies for conducting both practical on-site assessments and scientific laboratory examinations of earth for CSEB manufacturing and CSEB testing. In our manual we would like to point out two crucial questions that help with the identification:

1) Is the earth free of organic components? The presence of organic matter renders the earth unsuitable, as its decomposition compromises the stability of the material for construction purposes. It is imperative to procure earth from beneath the topsoil layer to minimize the presence of biological activity and organic content.

2) Does the earth exhibit a significant proportion of clay? Upon moistening, the earth sample should become plastic and formable, indicating the presence of clay. This plasticity allows the initially loose earth to be molded into cohesive shapes like spheres without fragmentation.

Sourcing Earth

Suitable soil can often be sourced as a by-product of other activities. Commonly the excavation material from basement constructions has been used for these purposes. However, as we discourage the construction of basements due to their substantial reliance on energy-intensive materials such as steel and concrete; excavation material from building sites is not considered in this manual. Nonetheless, other activities such as sand and gravel mining often extract loamy soil as a by-product in vast and homogenous quantities. In the case of Studio Suddo Neuve, we identified a borrow site that provided material for road substructures. With the advantages of having accessibility for trucks and an excavation depth that precluded the presence of organic components, the pit has been supplying soil for our earth-block manufacturing in Mako. ●24

II Manufacturing CSEBs

On-site block manufacturing often proves more challenging than anticipated. The storage and processing of earth, the actual block-making process, and particularly the curing and storage of blocks, entail significant space requirements that are seldom available in urban contexts. Recognizing the aim of a systemic transformation in construction through the utilization of CSEBs—that is, intending to extend beyond the construction of a demonstration buildings—we chose to develop our block-manufacturing site as a long-term facility. Beyond block making, this permanent manufacturing site is also used to test full-scale prototypes and investigate structural questions in the form of practical experiments.

Set up of a CSEB Manufactory

Flat terrain provides an optimal starting point for a site, as it allows for the establishment of the various manufacturing stages without the need for complex landscaping. Accessibility to the site by trucks is crucial for the delivery of earth and the subsequent dispatch of blocks. Depending on the existing infrastructure, it is necessary to assess whether water can be sourced on site through public infrastructure or wells, as the pressing and curing of CSEBs requires substantial amounts of processing water. For the organization, maintenance, and nightly securing of tools, we recommend a small workshop building. Depending on the targeted manufacturing volume, sufficient space should be allocated for the storage of raw earth, sieving and

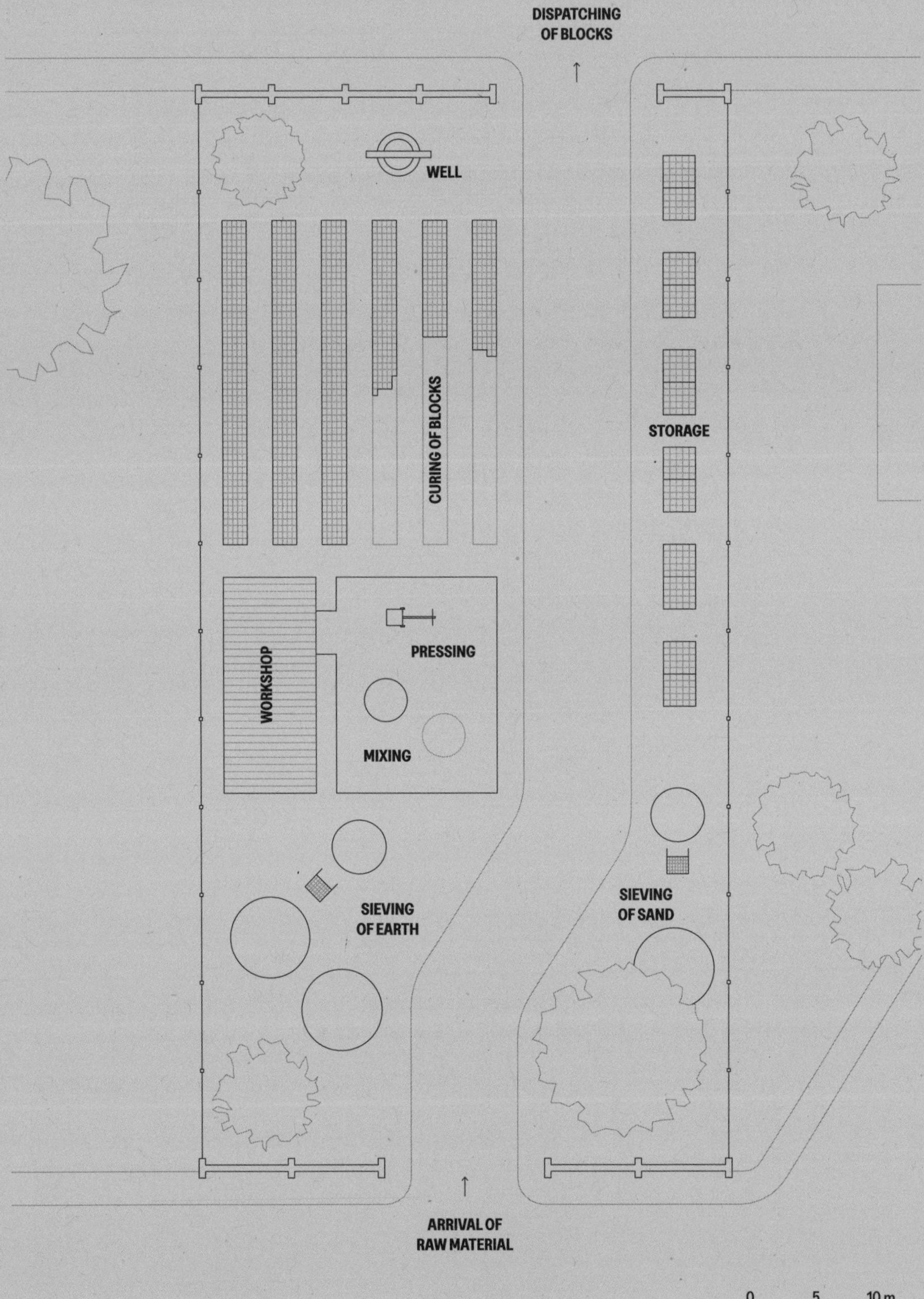

● 25 Set Up of Earth Block Manufactory

mixing earth, block pressing, curing of freshly pressed blocks, and storage of blocks for sale. Studio Suddo Neuve operates on a manufacturing site of 400 square meters and can process approximately 15,000 blocks per production cycle.

A block press serves as the pivotal element of the manufacturing site. There is a range of options available from various producers, with manual block presses being the most prevalent and affordable. These manual presses benefit from mechanical leverage, significantly amplifying the applied human force. In locations with sufficient infrastructure and higher labor cost, semi- and fully automatic machines represent an alternative, offering streamlined production processes and substantially higher output capacities. When choosing a press, we recommend matching the desired production output with the capability of the press and the availability of trained personal to operate and maintain the machines. In manual production, it is also important to consider that it is physically demanding, requiring either multiple production teams or longer break periods. The sometimes extreme price differences for seemingly identical presses do reflect their quality. The cheapest options are designed for building a single house and are likely to wear out after just one season. On the other hand, the manufacturers offering more expensive presses prioritize durability and the possibility of independent repairs with universally available parts and simple welding work. Another important quality feature is the pressure exerted by the press onto the earth, which correlates directly to the respective compressive strength of the yielded blocks. Good manual presses are usually operated by two people and achieve a pressure of 15 tons; for a block measuring 29.5 cm × 14 cm × 9 cm, this translates to approximately 35 bars. (Semi-) automated presses typically exceed this and result in even better compressed blocks. However, the required pressure varies based on the composition of the soil and can be adjusted by fine-tuning the volume of earth that is loaded into the pressing chamber. ●25

Sieving Earth

The preparation of earth for producing CSEBs seeks to achieve two primary objectives. Firstly, it aims to homogenize the earth. Secondly, it involves optimizing the composition of the earth by adding and/or subtracting individual components.

During the transportation and unloading phases, the finer components of the earth settle toward the bottom, while gravel and coarse sand remain on the surface. To homogenize the earth, it is sieved. Here, particles larger than 10 millimeters, such as rocks and larger debris, are eliminated resulting in a consistently mixed source material ready for further processing. Depending on the infrastructure of a project, the utilization of mechanical grinding or hammering machines presents an alternative approach and is especially useful if the earth naturally forms lumps. Instead of simply sieving out rocks, these machines effectively pulverize them into fine grit, seamlessly integrating them into the earth. Sieving and potentially grinding the earth are integral components of the production logistics. They involve moving the earth from the delivery area toward the block press to create space for new deliveries and minimize the distance the earth must travel for further processing. ●26

●26 Sieving of Earth for the Production of CSEBs

Optimizing and Mixing Materials

While sieving earth and sand can be conducted independently of block pressing, optimizing and mixing mark the start of a comprehensive CSEB manufacturing chain from source material to block. The complexity of optimizing the earth varies depending on its natural composition. The earth utilized by Studio Suddo Neuve belongs to the laterite family, characterized by a predominance of fine composites (silt and clay), along with coarse gravel and small rocks. It exhibits a low content of sand. In our case, achieving a balanced distribution of fines, sand, and gravel involves adding one part of sand to every two parts of laterite, thereby aligning the overall composition with the previously discussed benchmarks. ●27 As explained in the previous chapter, while producing non-stabilized blocks offers further environmental and potential economic benefits, stabilizing the blocks with an additional binding agent, such as fly ash or cement, enhances their water resistance and enables the construction of monolithic, low-maintenance structures. Studio Suddo Neuve employs 6 mass percent of cement as a stabilizer. After thoroughly combining sand and laterite, the stabilizer is added.

It is important to develop practical measuring rules that make the process of mixing efficient. Measuring the composites in multiples of wheelbarrows and buckets is much easier to track while serving as a means of quality control that can easily be executed. In practical terms, one bag of cement (35 liters) is mixed with four wheelbarrows of laterite (each containing 80 liters) and two wheelbarrows of sand (each containing 80 liters). A clean platform is recommendable for the mixing process to not dilute the mixing ratios with additional soil from the ground. Initially, the masses are dry mixed. During a third mixing cycle, six buckets of water (each containing 10 liters) are added to activate the clay minerals and the hydraulic stabilizer. The water content is maintained at a relatively low level, but the amount of water added is highly dependent on the moisture level of the raw ingredients and needs to be adjusted accordingly. It is crucial to prevent the material from reaching a muddy consistency. Instead, enough water needs to be added to achieve an earth-moist state. Determining the right amount of water requires a certain level of experience and can only be assessed after a few blocks have been manufactured and tested. With increasing familiarity with the material, the appropriate water content can be monitored through observing color tone and consistency while mixing.

● 27 Optimizing and Mixing Materials

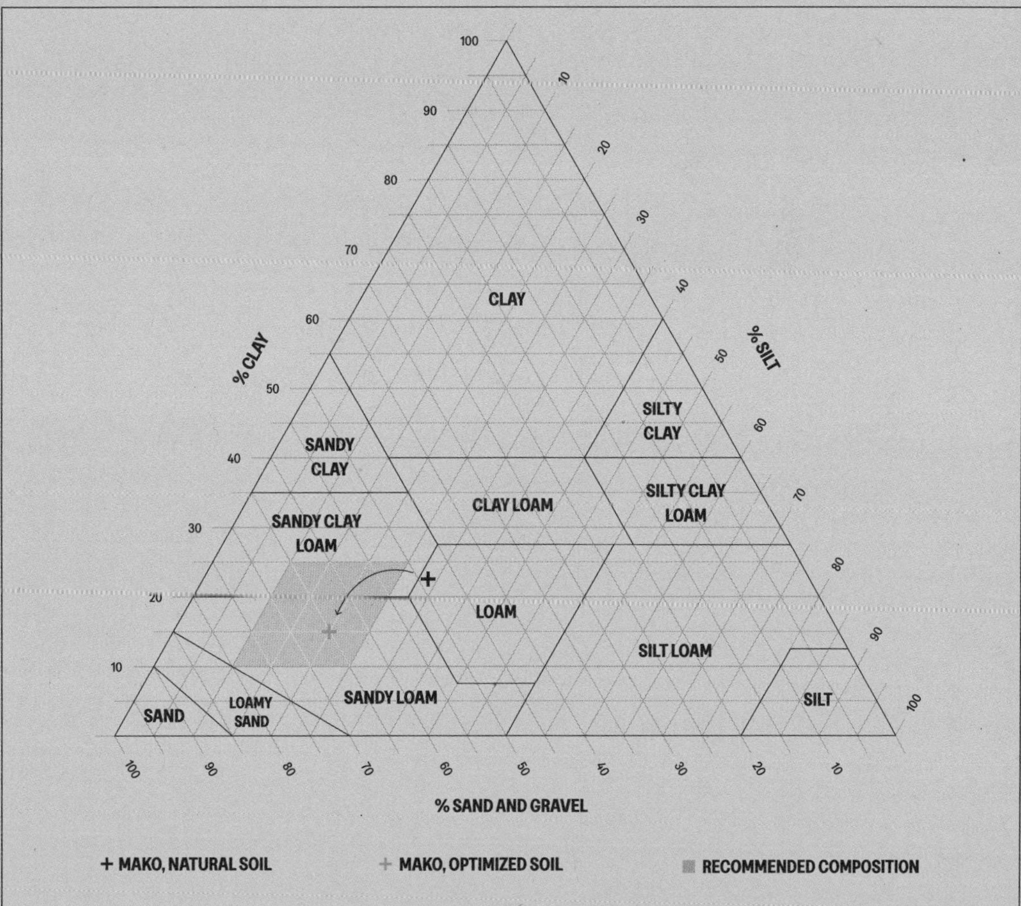

Block Production

Pressing blocks involves three stages: charging, compressing, and ejecting. Here, establishing and maintaining a consistent working rhythm is paramount. Given the sequence of straightforward yet physically demanding tasks, achieving a harmonious balance between the number of workers per station and the rotation of workers among stations is crucial. A common working rhythm ensures the uninterrupted operation of all stations at a synchronized pace.

In charging the block press, it is essential to incorporate a measuring mechanism that ensures a consistent supply. Just as with measuring the raw materials, it is advisable to implement a practical solution such as a charging shovel or bucket that indicates a defined volume. However, even slight variations in water content can significantly affect the mixture's density, which make the method of filling by volume prone to errors. Particularly in the developmental stages of a CSEB manufacturing line, it can be beneficial to validate the loading process through weight. While this process may be slower, it can later be converted to volume-based loading. We recommend two workers for charging. One worker is tasked with loading the charging shovel, while the other monitors the moisture levels of the mixture and conducts any necessary adjustments.

For compression, up to three workers may be required to operate a press depending on the type. Studio Suddo Neuve utilizes an Indian-made block press called Auram 3000. In this setup, one of the three workers is responsible for placing the pre-measured mixture into the press's mold, closing the lid, and locking the press for compression. Following this, two workers operate a lever arm connected to the bottom plate of the mold. By moving this bottom plate against the locked-in earth, they compress the material to form a block. This phase represents the most challenging aspect of the manufacturing chain and demands synchronized efforts to effectively utilize the worker's force. Compared to hand-molded adobe and other earth-based building techniques like cob or rammed earth, the compression of stabilized earth in a block press yields significantly denser, and more dimensionally uniform results. ●28

The block-pressing process concludes with the ejection of the block from the press. The mold's lid is pushed open, and as the lever arm is returned to its initial position for the next compression, the bottom plate moves upward, ejecting the manufactured block for retrieval. To measure the quality of the yielded block, two on-site tests are conducted. The first one involves checking the dimensions. While length and width are predefined by the mold, the height varies and depends on the set-up of the machine as well as the charging weight/volume and moisture level of the soil. To prevent problems during the masonry work, the blocks should limit the variable in block height to ±2 millimeters. In a second test, the compressive strengths of the freshly manufactured block can be checked with a penetrometer test. This tool utilizes a spring-loaded metal pin to press against the surface of the block and measures the pressure at which it penetrates the block. Freshly pressed blocks should withstand penetration until a pressure of at least 4.5 kilogram per square centimeter. Passing this test indicates the block's suitability for multistory construction in terms of its compressive strength. Quality control should be seamlessly integrated into the working rhythm on a regular basis. After every twenty blocks, the team of workers can take a brief break while conducting the control checks. In the event of any irregularities, the blocks manufactured since the last successful testing are returned, crushed and blended back into the earth mixture. At Studio Suddo Neuve, after several months of experimentation, the pressing rate reached several blocks per working minute, totaling up to 800 blocks per working day.

Block presses can manufacture various types of blocks. Among the most prevalent are full and half blocks, integral in erecting both single- and multistory walls. Through their combination, they simplify the creation of apertures within walls as well as the construction of walls with varying thicknesses. Moreover, specialized blocks, including U-shaped ring beam blocks and hollow blocks, designed for electrical cable installation, can be produced. Especially noteworthy are ceiling blocks, which are suitable for floor slab construction. These are suspended between two load-bearing beams, an earth-block component that we will address later in this manual *(→ p. 84)*.

● **28 Block Production with a Manual Press**

●29 Stacking and Curing

Stacking and Curing

After a block is ejected from the machine, a worker retrieves and transports it to the site's stacking area, the last step of block making. Although the blocks are relatively stable in form at this stage, their edges remain vulnerable to breakage. It is crucial to lift the blocks by using the heel of the hand to apply pressure to the center of the block. Reducing overall space requirements, it is possible to stack them up to four blocks high. Since stacking requires careful handling and often involves walking longer distances, a second person is necessary to ensure that ejected blocks are promptly removed from the press, maximizing manufacturing output. To attain optimal quality, it is imperative to avoid rapid vaporization of the water and ensure that the blocks are curing. Thus, covering the blocks with mats or sheets is recommended. Furthermore, on days with elevated temperatures, watering the blocks to replenish evaporated water is recommended. ●29

III Assessment of CSEBs

Similar to the examination of earth samples, numerous resources offer guidance on evaluating CSEBs. This manual will outline procedures for testing the key parameters around compressive strength, quantifying mass loss from water immersion, and analyzing the effects of rising damp. The testing frameworks are explained with reference to the DIN 18945, the German Industry Standard for earth blocks (2018). If CSEBs are to be sold as a building product to third parties, it is recommended to have the performance of the blocks evaluated by a specialized testing facility. However, many tests can be conducted independently and without significant investment into costly laboratory equipment, providing insights into strengths, limitations, and any optimization opportunities.

Tests are best conducted on conditioned blocks that have achieved constant weight over a prolonged period under controlled temperature and humidity conditions. Adequate conditioning is indicated by minimal weight variance, typically within single-digit grams, observed over at least two consecutive days. The DIN 18945 recommends to test blocks at 23 degrees Celsius and 50 percent relative humidity allowing for fluctuations of ±5 degrees Celsius in temperature and ±15 percent in humidity for in-house testing. After constant weight has been attained, the final dimensions and weight of the blocks are measured. To ensure the overall validity of the obtained values, both assessments should be performed on a minimum of five randomly selected blocks. CSEBs exhibit negligible shrinkage between the pressing and setting phases, resulting in final dimensions that closely mirror those recorded immediately after pressing. Meanwhile, the weight of conditioned CSEBs in relation to their volume provides information about their density (noted in kilograms per cubic meter). The blocks of Studio Suddo Neuve exhibit a density of approximately 1,900 kilograms per cubic meter, positioning them within the intermediate spectrum for CSEBs, which commonly ranges from 1,500 to 2,200 kilograms per cubic meter. A wide variance in the weight of sampled blocks from the same batch indicates inconsistency in the loading process, a homogenously performing product can only ensue if variance in mass is minimized.

Compressive Strength

Determining the compressive strength of CSEBs enables the dimensioning of earth masonry walls according to their expected load. Conventional guidelines provided by press manufacturers often suggest that arranging blocks in a stretcher bond permits load-bearing masonry of up to two stories, while utilizing a running bond is conducive to non-load-bearing masonry. However, these guidelines overlook the inherent quality variation among CSEBs. It is plausible for some blocks to surpass these expectations, whereas others may generally lack the structural integrity required for load-bearing construction.

The process of determining compressive strength involves subjecting CSEBs to uniaxial pressure, exerted perpendicular to the block's surface using a compression testing machine. The rate of loading should be constant

●30 Compressive Strength Test of CSEB

and selected to ensure that the blocks fracture no earlier than thirty seconds after the onset of loading. The test is carried out until the blocks fracture, and the maximum stress is recorded. Once a series of blocks have undergone testing, their results are averaged. Depending on the raw materials, stabilizers, and processing techniques, CSEBs exhibit a wide range of compressive strengths, ranging from as low as 1 megapascal to 8 megapascals and more. Different building codes require different minimal compressive strength for load-bearing applications; most countries require a minimum of 2.5 megapascals for load-bearing CSEBs. Comparing these values to the performance of concrete or fired blocks, it becomes clear that CSEBs are slightly weaker, leading to thicker wall dimensions than conventional alternatives. However, the increase in wall thickness results in a greater overall thermal mass, a common weak point of conventional construction techniques. ●30

Moisture Tests

Although stabilizing earthen blocks with additives such as fly ash or cement enhances their water resistance, it is important to verify their actual moisture behavior through simulated stresses. Research has found the relationship between relative humidity and compressive strength of earth blocks to be linear, translating to an eventual failure of the blocks with high moisture levels. Hence the performance of blocks in respect to moisture exposure becomes essential, especially if pure CEBs are used.

During an immersion test, the extent of the blocks' mass loss upon direct contact with water is determined. In practice, this test can be compared to the impact of rain on exposed exterior masonry. For the test setup, a minimum of three conditioned CSEBs are held vertically in water to a depth of 10 centimeters for ten minutes. Subsequently, the water is evaporated in an oven, and the residue is weighed. CSEBs are expected to pass this test with minimal residue. If they exhibit a mass loss of over five percentage points, they should not be used for exposed exterior masonry. In such cases, the manufacturing of the blocks needs to be revised. Specifically, adjusting the proportion of cement and the compression of the blocks in the press can enhance the blocks' performance. Significant variations in the results imply that the production was not carried out under consistent standards.

Rising damp describes the phenomenon where moisture present in the building ground ascends upwards through the capillary action of the foundation and masonry, accumulating in the plinth and walls. This can lead to cracking and, depending on the resilience of the load-bearing materials, may compromise the structural integrity of a building. Here, too, the stabilization of the blocks enhances their resistance to potential softening caused by rising damp and the degree of this increased resistance can be determined through a simulated test. The test requires a large tray that can be filled with water. For the test, at least three CSEBs are placed on a base made of capillary-conductive bricks overlaid with sponge cloths. The tray is filled with water up to just below the top of the capillary-conductive bricks, allowing moisture to ascend through the sponge cloths into the CSEBs located in the area not surrounded by water. Over the course of twenty-four hours, the blocks are observed to determine if there are visible cracks caused by swelling on the top and side surfaces of the blocks. Vertical cracks indicate failure, suggesting a need to revise both formula and manufacturing techniques.

Earth Mortar and Render

The construction of masonry requires two primary materials: blocks and mortar. While the manufacturing of blocks is quite complex, producing the complementary mortar is significantly simpler. Just like the blocks, it is made up of a mixture of earth, sand, and cement. Hence, the source material can be obtained and prepared during the material processing for the blocks. Depending on the desired joint pattern of the masonry, it can be beneficial to further refine the earth by sieving it through a 5–8-millimeter sieve to reduce the maximum grain size and facilitate the leveling process of blocks during laying. Typically, the mortar is prepared on site, and the speed of preparation is adjusted to the pace of construction. At Studio Suddo Neuve we manually mix the mortar in a wheelbarrow. Here, four buckets of earth are combined with two buckets of sand and five liters of cement (approximately 7.5 kilograms) before being blended with around 10 liters of water. In comparison to the mixture used for block pressing, the mortar has a higher moisture content, with a creamy consistency.

A third material that can be used for the finishing of the masonry surface is an earth render. This is not to be confused with a multi-millimeter-thick layer of plaster. Instead, it serves as a method to achieve level joints and blocks by filling in gaps and smoothing broken edges. In this process, the mortar material undergoes additional sieving. Textiles with meshes finer than 2 millimeters are required to obtain a very fine powder suitable for this purpose.

IV Building with CSEBs

When designing a CSEB building it becomes apparent that CSEBs alone are insufficient for constructing an entire building, much like any other material. Foundations play a crucial role in supporting the weight of the robust earth construction, while openings are left for doors and windows. Constructing floor slabs and roofs presents challenges that require materials that can span larger distances. Additionally, installations are positioned to supply the structure with water and electricity and, depending on the building's purpose, flooring and wall finishes are selected to enhance user comfort. Rather than investigating mono-material construction solutions, the focus shifts to maximizing the utilization of CSEBs while exploring helpful symbioses with additional materials. ●31

In contrast to certain international practices, where CSEBs are merely utilized as in-fill material for a reinforced concrete skeleton, CSEBs alone are capable of creating load-bearing and bracing structures. To meet these requirements, it is necessary to consider the fundamental principles of masonry. This includes adequately

● 31 Full-Scale Prototype of a Floor Slab

dimensioned wall thickness, adhering to maximum wall heights and lengths, and interlocking the blocks through masonry bonds. Particularly around doors and windows, attention must be paid to distributing overhead loads through ring beams. Longer walls without bracing from adjacent cross walls may need reinforcement through rigid columns. CSEB structures benefit from a monolithic construction method, where the raw structure equals the finished building in large part and only requires minimal revision later on. Therefore, meticulous attention must be paid to the intended dimensions during masonry production, and the handling of the blocks must be conducted with great care to avoid unnecessary surface damage. Bulging masonry, broken corners, and slanted wall openings can be difficult or impossible to correct later.

Designing CSEBs Structures

With their superior dimensional uniformity compared to hand-molded adobe, CSEBs allow for precise project planning prior to construction. As with any masonry work, wall lengths, heights, and openings are determined by multiples of blocks and joints. Ensuring robust masonry bonds involves planning each masonry row separately, allowing insight into the necessary overall quantity of CSEBs and the distribution of different block types. To optimize material, time, and cost, not all walls need to be load-bearing; for instance, simple partition walls can utilize half blocks to reduce wall dimensions. Masons benefit from on-site plans indicating block patterns for each row. Furthermore, planning both floor plans and elevations serves as a starting point for other trades involved in construction. For example, carpenters and welders can commence prefabricating finishing elements like doors and windows, expediting the construction process. While not all projects require such meticulous planning, it's also feasible to establish rules of thumb for estimating material requirements. For instance, Studio Suddo Neuve calculates that forty full blocks are needed to construct one square meter of load-bearing wall surface. Multiplying this figure by the length and height of all walls required for a project provides the total number of CSEBs needed. However, this method lacks differentiation between block types (e.g., half and full blocks), which is dependent on factors such as the number of corners and angles and can therefore not be derived through this estimation. ●32

The following catalog of building details has been compiled over the years through various projects undertaken by Studio Suddo Neuve. Spanning from foundation to roof, it highlights the utilization of CSEBs and offers suggestions on where and how they can be effectively complemented by additional building materials. These proposed solutions have been developed within the framework of our work in Mako, drawing upon the expertise and materials available in that region. Many components rely on metalworking, which we have found to be a highly compatible combination with earth masonry. However, this preference also arises from the general scarcity of wood, limiting the use of bio-based materials, particularly in larger components such as floor and roof beams. The catalog is further enhanced by a series of photos from construction sites to provide context and insight into the building process.

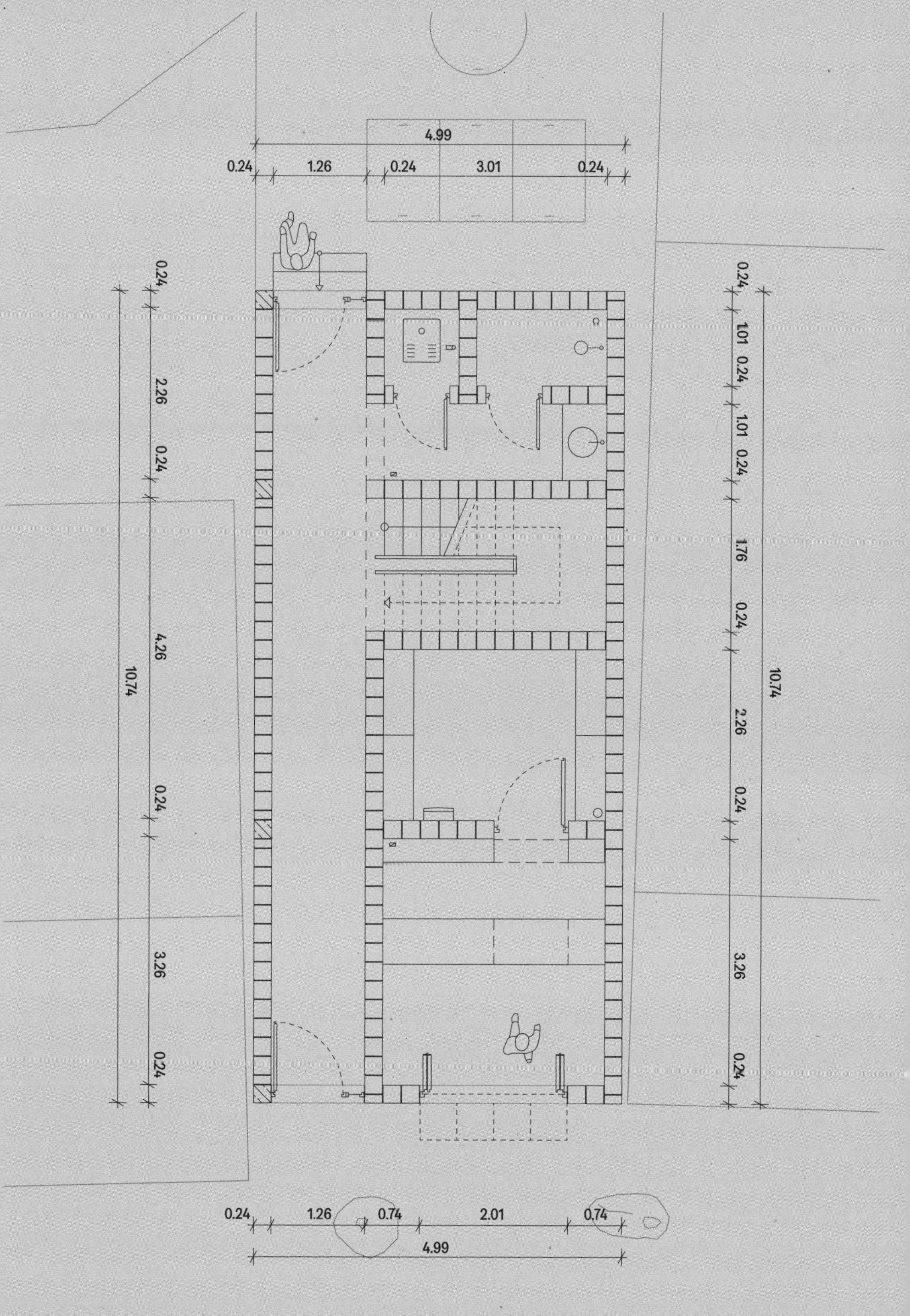
4.99
0.24
1.26
0.24
3.01
0.24
0.24
2.26
0.24
4.26
10.74
0.24
3.26
0.24
0.24
1.01
0.24
1.01
0.24
1.76
0.24
2.26
0.24
3.26
0.24
10.74
0.24
1.26
0.74
2.01
0.74
4.99

Foundation

A stable building ground and solid foundations are essential to support the immense loads of a CSEB construction. With a raw density of approximately 2 tons per cubic meter of masonry, above-average loads are applied, which need to be absorbed by the foundations. In urban contexts, it is crucial to ensure that neighboring buildings are not adversely affected by the loads of the CSEB construction. In our work we have used standard strip foundations made from reenforced concrete. To minimize the use of concrete, large rocks as aggregates were added to the base of the foundation.

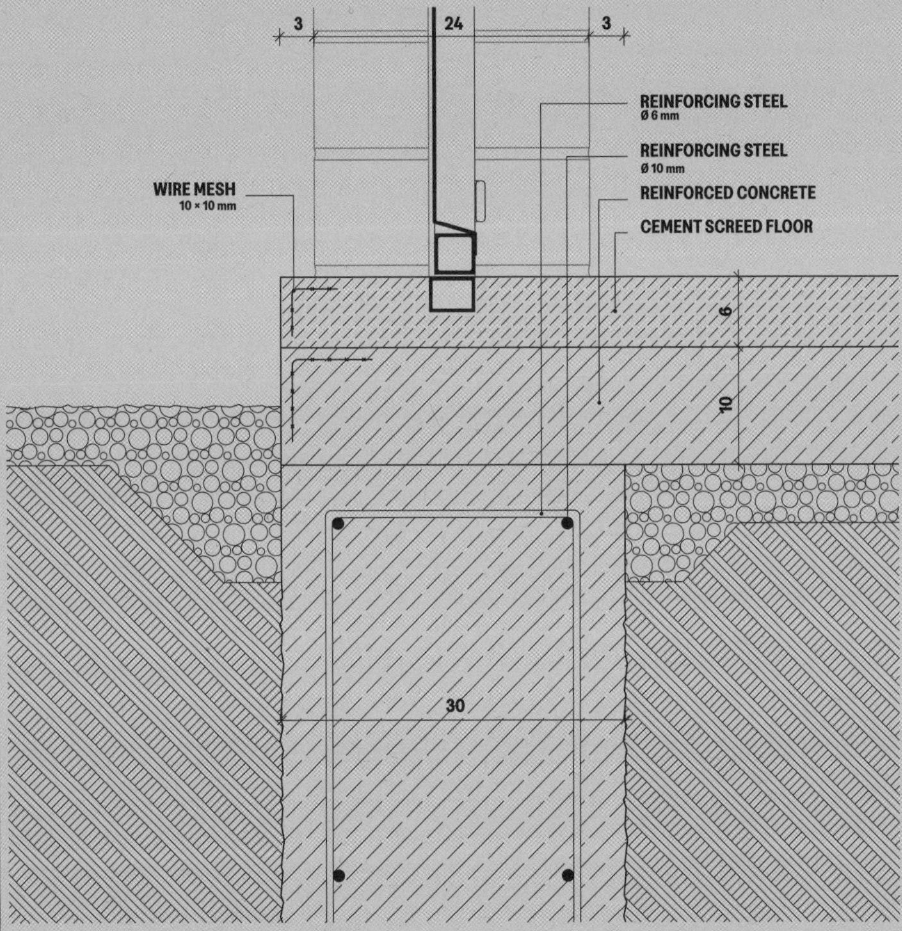

●33 Foundation Detail, Section

34 Preparation of Foundations

●35 Masonry Work

Walls

When constructing the masonry, teams of two people can work together. While one person ensures the availability of blocks, mortar, and tools, the second person lays and levels the blocks in the mortar bed. The blocks should be moistened before installation to prevent them from absorbing moisture of the mortar too quickly. Spacer bars can help maintain a uniform thickness of the bearing joints, ensuring a homogenous joint pattern.

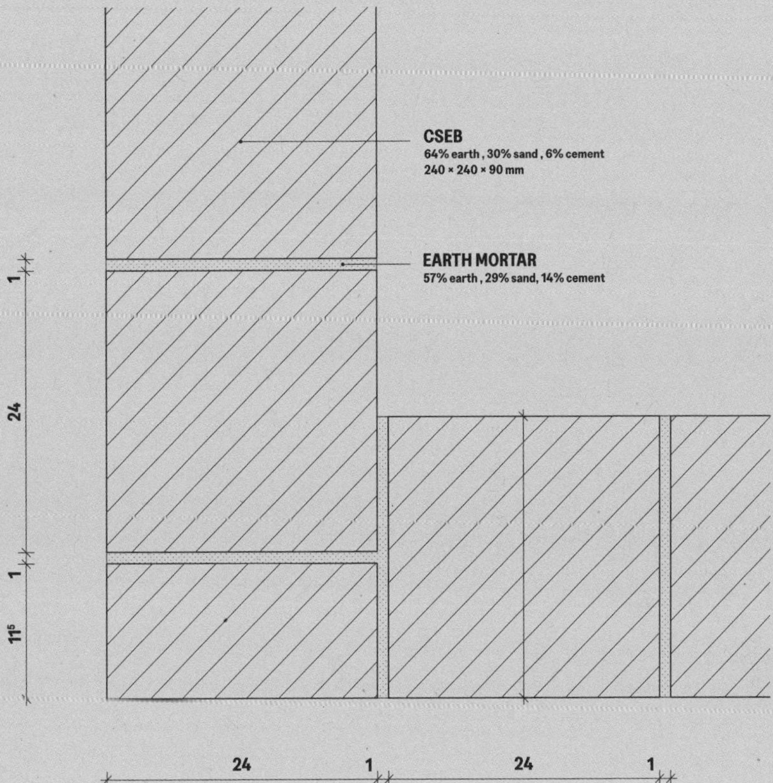

●36 **Load-Bearing CSEB Wall Detail, Floor Plan**

Floor Slab

It is possible to incorporate CSEBs in the construction of floor slabs. Ceiling blocks, also referred to as hourdis blocks, can be inserted into spanning beams, thus reducing the ecological footprint compared to concrete-only decks. Depending on availability, wooden beams can also be utilized for this purpose, further reducing the ecological impact of the component. Additionally, a load-distributing layer is necessary above the ceiling blocks to evenly distribute potential point loads across the area. The underside of the blocks can be cladded with an earth render. However, with a view to the dismantling of the construction, it is advantageous to leave them untreated.

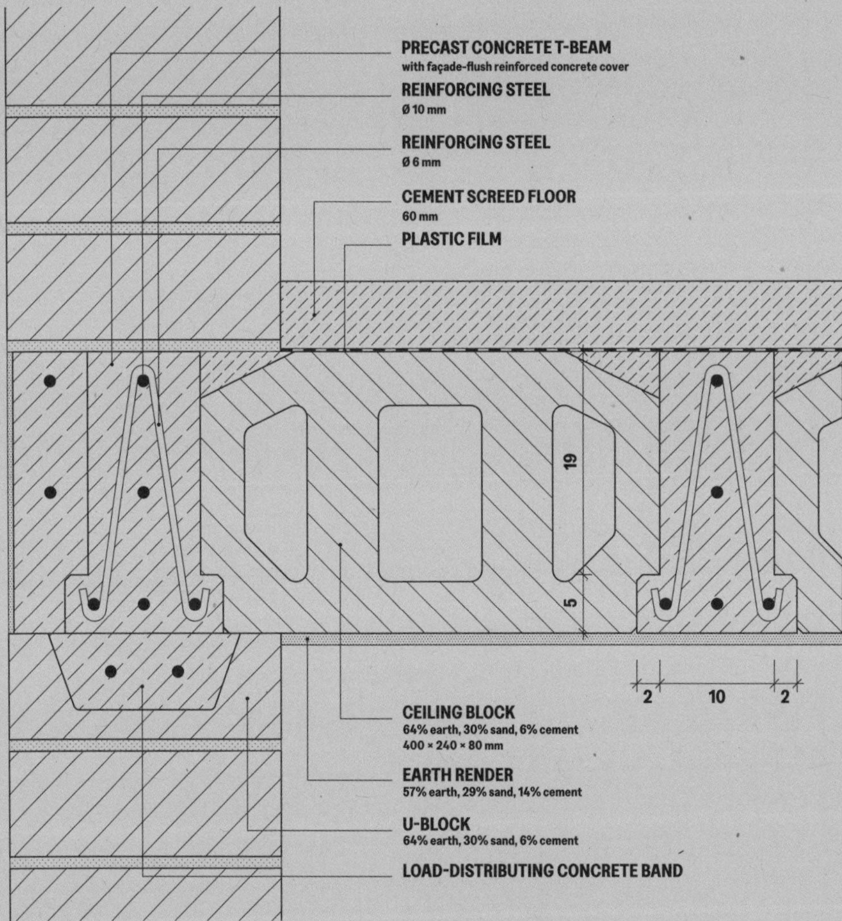

●37 Floor Slab Detail, Section

●38 Laying of Ceiling Blocks

39 Door Fabrication at a Welder Workshop

Doors

In regard to door installation, we have found that the door jamb threshold can be installed at ground level if it was previously recessed in the construction of the floor slab. The vertical door jambs are directly connected to the CSEB masonry, eliminating the need for extensive slotting work. To simplify construction, we recommend extending the openings up to the ring beam and, depending on the room height, preferably using a closed infill element in the upper part of the opening rather than adding an additional lintel directly above the opening.

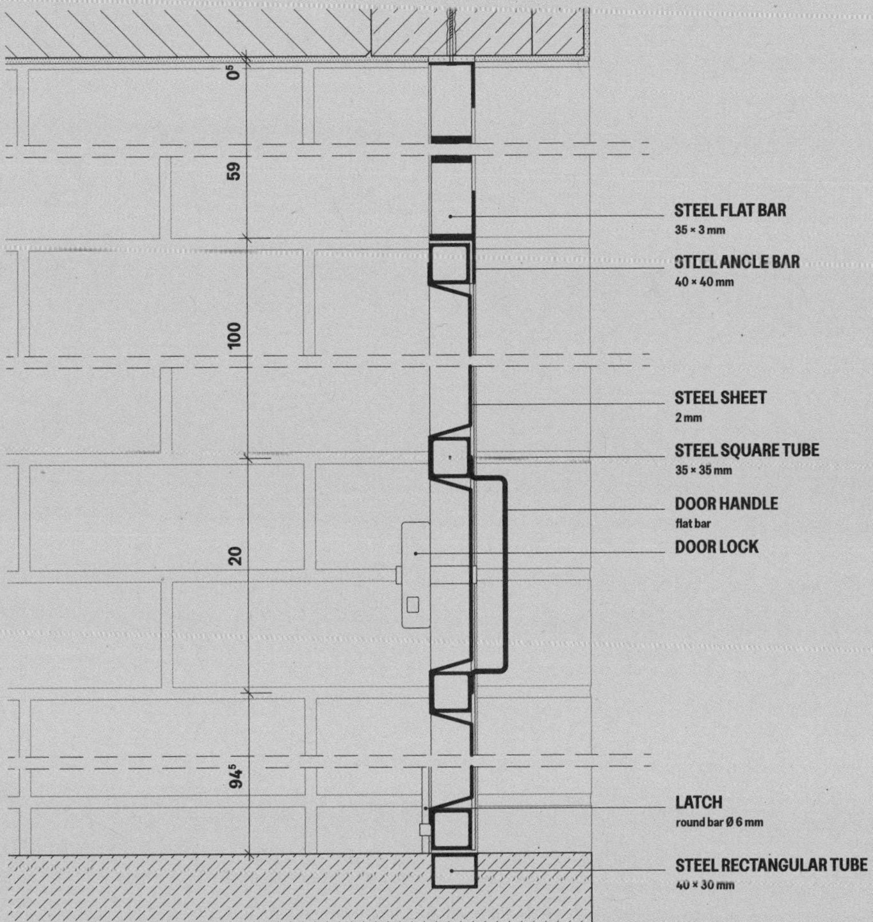

●40 Door Detail, Section

Windows

The installation of windows is similar to the installation of doors, with an anchorage of the window frame directly connected to the masonry. While it is not essential for all window elements to be operable, at least one window sash should open for ventilation. To minimize unnecessary heating of the interior space, window openings should be kept to a minimum and positioned to allow cross-ventilation.

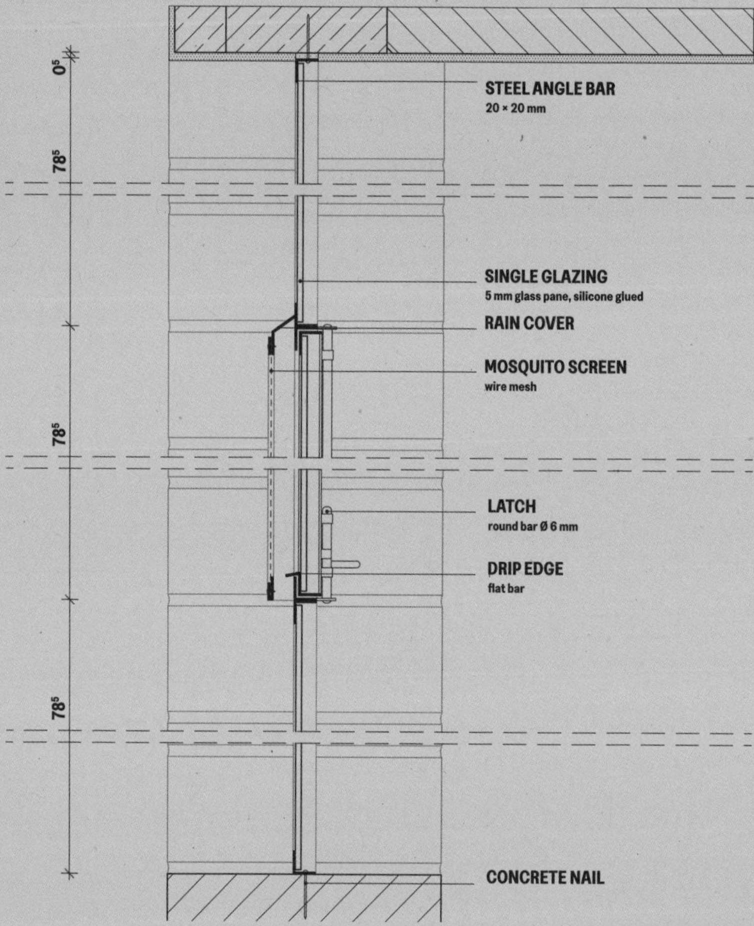

●41 Window Detail, Section

●42 Installation of Windows

● 43 Cable Duct with Socket and Light Switches

Electrical Installation

The installation of electrical wiring can be carried out without the need for slotting the masonry. For this purpose, a vertical column containing sockets and light switches is positioned directly in front of the masonry. The column can be threaded through the floor slab and also the roof of the building, allowing direct access to power from a PV system or the public grid. To supply ceiling lights, a cable can be run from the column into the floor slab and then routed on the upper side to the outlet of the lamp.

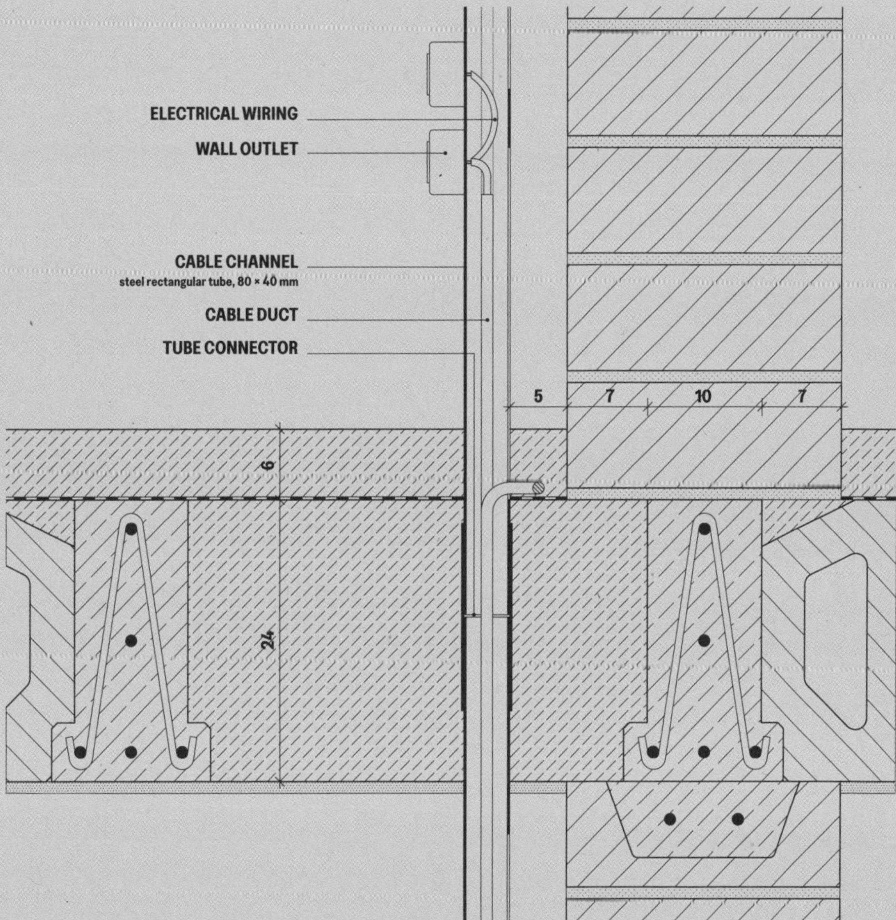

●44 Electrical Installation Detail, Section

Roof

When constructing roofs, another traditional method of earth-based construction can be utilized. Here, bamboo mats are placed between a framework of wooden or concrete beams and covered on the upper side with a layer of earth. The earth layer provides the structure with high thermal mass, insulating the interior spaces from excessive external heat. Depending on the pitch of the roof, the component is completed with either a layer of corrugated metal sheets (flat roof) or with thatch (pitched roof).

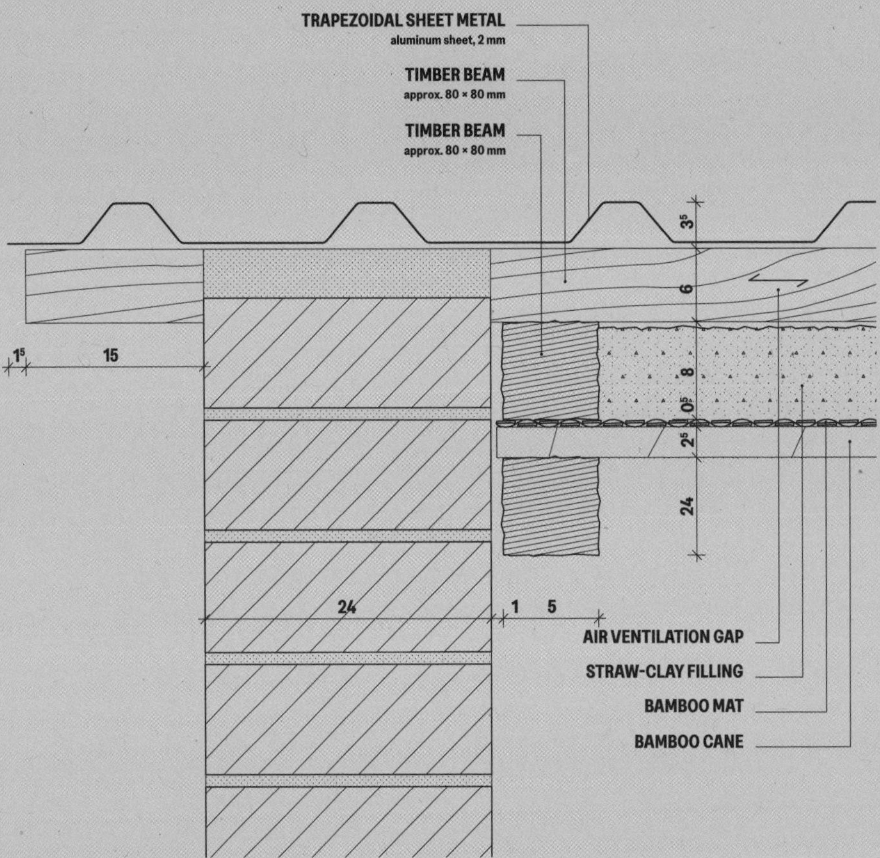

●45 Roof Detail, Section

●46 Construction of a Bamboo-Earth-Hybrid Roof

V Maintenance and Deconstruction

The more a component is exposed to the elements, the more it wears and requires maintenance. By design, CSEB construction is resistant to moisture and frost, but the much less compacted mortar of CSEB masonry often struggles to perform at the same level as the blocks. In our experience, highly exposed areas of CSEB façades require regular maintenance, such as brushing and washing surfaces that suffer from algae growth. While we have opted for visible masonry both in- and outside, it is also possible to plaster the walls. For the exterior, lime-based plasters that can withstand weather conditions are ideal. For the interior, pure earth plaster is recommended, as the physical properties of raw earth create a particularly good interior climate. Visible damages from screw holes and such can easily be filled with mortar again and often repairs blend in texture and color without any special treatment or replastering of large surfaces.

When CSEB buildings are dismantled, blocks and mortar can be recycled to produce new building materials. This is done by crushing the reclaimed material and using it as raw material for a new CSEBs or mortar. Since the setting reaction of cement is irreversible, fresh cement must be added to the recovered materials. The reuse of reclaimed CSEBs and mortar as the starting point for a new generation of products is the ideal type of recycling, since even in their crushed state they do not have the same properties as the materials in their natural state. Although crushed CSEBs can be left in nature without risk, the material lacks the binding properties of the clay minerals that were present at the outset. In contrast, CEBs, cement-free compressed earth blocks, can be used to make new CEBs without the addition of a hydraulic binder and can be returned to nature without any alterations to its composition.

Outcomes

Demonstration, Replication, Adaptation

Transitioning from experimentation with earth blocks to the exploration of their application in three-dimensional spaces, the research efforts shift toward visible design iterations. Demonstration buildings allow for the evaluation of CSEB architecture by the parameters of form, functionality, and performance. Here, the public acceptance and potential demand for CSEB structures hinge on their competitiveness with conventional alternatives, requiring both aesthetic appeal and functionalism to leverage the environmental advantages of earth blocks.

Following this approach, Studio Suddo Neuve initiated the construction of a pioneer demonstration building in June 2019. Located adjacent to the main road in Mako, this two-story construction incorporates a ground-floor commercial storefront and upper-floor residential spaces. Internal circulation is facilitated by a central corridor, which provides access to a staircase, wet rooms, and the courtyard. The upper level comprises a terrace and a single-room apartment, with the potential for incremental expansion through the construction of an additional bedroom. The courtyard offers outdoor space and maintenance access to the infrastructure for sewage water treatment and filtration; the demonstration building was the first in Mako with interior piping connected to the newly built central water system. The programmatic split of the project between housing and commercial use facilitates the demonstration of diverse spatial configurations and technically and structurally advanced constructions, such as wet rooms, staircases, and sewage systems. Further, the shop unit ensures continuous public accessibility to the interior of the CSEB structure.

Co-financed by the German Federal Ministry for Economic Cooperation and Development and the building plot owner, the construction of the project concluded in spring 2020. Functioning as a reference point for builders interested in the construction with CSEBs, the demonstration building has since supported Studio Suddo Neuve's vision to systemically integrate earth-based building products into the local construction industry. Additionally, this first intervention functions as a larger-scale living laboratory, where maintenance needs are monitored and addressed to inform better planning strategies for future projects. ●47

The construction process and the use of the demonstration building shifted the advantageous environmental performance of CSEBs to the background, adding practical parameters to the evaluation. The relatively small size of CSEBs compared to hollow concrete blocks results in a slower block-laying pace. While an experienced mason lays around 2.5 square meters of concrete-block wall surface per day, that same mason would lay only 1.5 square meters of CSEBs over the same period. However, due to the load-bearing capacities of earth masonry, no additional concrete columns need to be poured, resulting in comparable construction times. Moreover, the CSEBs' dimensional accuracy and subsequent precise masonry reduces the need for extensive reworking, plastering, and painting, further saving time and costs. Similarly, the integration of additional building components and materials—such as steel and timber for staircases, windows, and doors—proved to be seamless due to the accuracy of the masonry. This interface often poses challenges and tedious reworking processes as the openings in the rough concrete masonry are rarely at right angles.

While CSEB masonry's superior mass and wall thickness negatively affects the speed of bricklaying, it has a positive impact on thermal comfort. The density of CSEBs of 1,900 kilograms per cubic meter results in a mass of 456 kilograms per square meter of wall surface compared to the lighter concrete blocks with a density of 1,750 kilograms per cubic meter and a mass of 332.5 kilograms per square meter of wall surface. Hence, the CSEBs are much more efficient at insulating. Especially in the dry season, CSEB architecture has

●47 Pioneer Demonstration Building, Street View

● 48 Pioneer Demonstration Building, Staircase

convinced many with its notably cooler interior spaces. Similar findings have been scientifically confirmed, recording close to 20 percent fewer hours of heat discomfort in CSEB buildings compared to hollow concrete buildings in arid climates.[50] ●48

Due to the relative success of the first demonstration building, a number of interested builders approached Studio Suddo Neuve with a desire to employ Mako-made CSEBs in their construction projects. While the studio had been responsible for the planning and execution of the pioneer demonstration project, we recently started focusing on developing competencies in the manufacturing of CSEBs at scale and advising on CSEB applications rather than conceiving full construction projects. For the determination of necessary quantities, it remains essential to make plans at a 1:100 scale *(→ p. 79)*, while the final design and execution are delegated to the builders and their masons. In recent years, around ten buildings were independently realized in Mako and the wider region. A wide range of different typologies, ranging from school buildings and residential spaces to storage and animal sheds, have interpreted CSEBs and established their aesthetics in the Mako townscape *(→ p. 118–19)* for an overview of realized CSEB structures in Mako).

In the independent reproduction of earth-based structures, varying degrees of trust in the developed building system can be observed. While some buildings have relied on the familiar system of structure and infill —similar to building with hollow concrete blocks, where a skeleton of concrete columns and beams is filled with blocks—others have trusted in load bearing masonry structures. More generally, the follow-up projects demonstrate that the developed blocks can be, with some adjustments, integrated into the existing construction infrastructure and therefore substitute energy-intensive conventional solutions *(→ pp. 110–17)*. ●49 ●50

An initial degree of skepticism toward CSEBs can be attributed to the common dismissal of earth-based materials as impoverished and inferior.[51] Still today, Studio Suddo Neuve is challenged to overcome these prejudices, which continue to dissolve with the sustained aesthetic appeal and structural integrity of the first demonstration buildings. This trend is strengthened by learnings from and improvements of realized projects, which allow CSEBs to be incorporated into an increasingly wider variety of typologies with more challenging applications. In this, a major advantage of earth blocks is the modularity of the masonry unit itself that can be adjusted to the specific spatial requirements of each project. More pragmatically, the growing utilization of CSEB structures substantiates the notion that

50 Hassane Seini Moussa et al., "Comparative Study of Thermal Comfort Induced from Masonry Made of Stabilized Compressed Earth Block vs Conventional Cementitious Material," *Journal of Minerals and Materials Characterization and Engineering* 7, no. 6 (2019): 385–403.

51 For a more detailed and global analysis on the unfavorable associations of earth architecture see: Alastair T. M. Marsh and Yask Kulshreshtha, "The State of Earthen Housing Worldwide: How Development Affects Attitudes and Adoption," *Building Research & Information* 50, no. 5 (July 4, 2022): 485–501.

● 49 Hybrid Construction: Corner Store ● 50 CSEB Construction: One-Room Housing Unit

earth-based materials yield robust and durable building solutions, capable of conforming to contemporary architectural demands. However, we consider the successful integration of CSEBs into the architectural production in Mako only as an intermediate step and continue to experiment with CEBs to eventually substitute large portions of CSEBs with an even higher performing material. The following analysis demonstrates the cost (economically and environmental) saving potentials of the different building materials. ●51

Balance Sheets

Contrary to the impression that in an era of global capitalism, sustainable products are a privilege of the academic elites, our experience shows that re-entangling Mako's urbanization with earth instead of concrete proves to be economically viable. This can be demonstrated using the model of a typical, single-story, two-room house (48 square meters of floor space). For the comparison, the material requirements of the dis-

●51 Axonometries of Realized CSEB Constructions ***(→ pp. 118–19)***

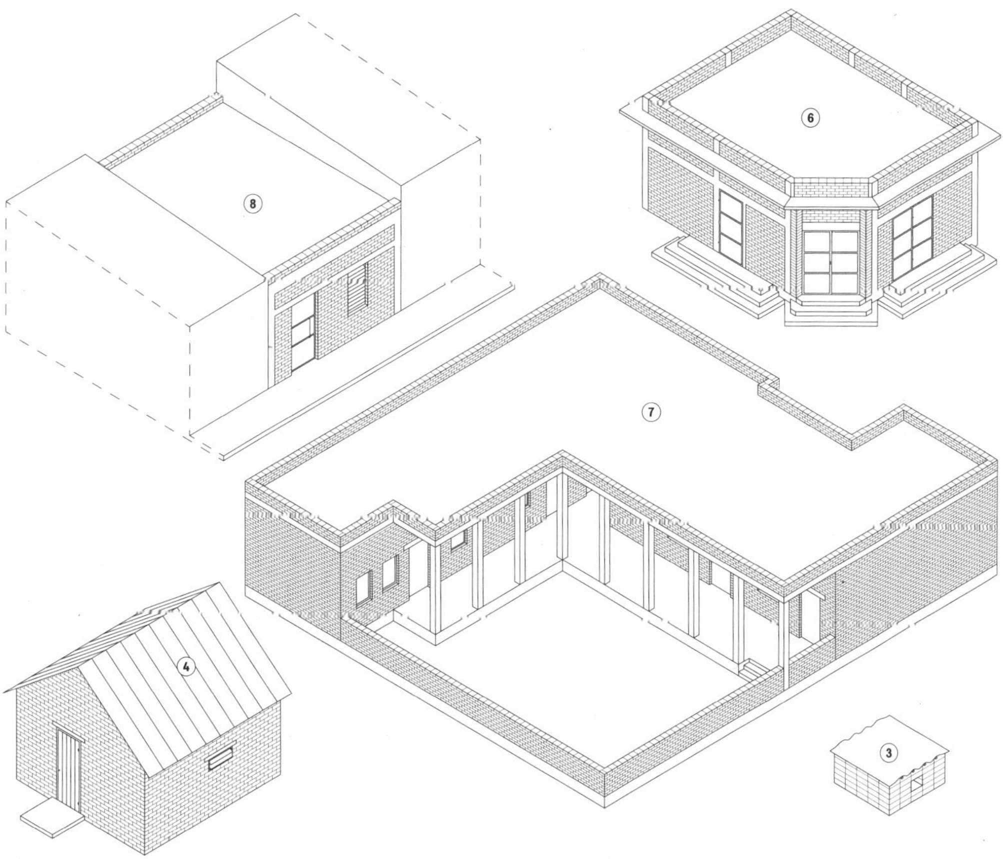

③ HENHOUSE ④ ONE-ROOM HOUSING UNIT ⑥ CORNER STORE ⑦ BUNGALOW RESIDENCE ⑧ CLASSROOM

52 Our findings on the cost and life-cycle cost of CSEBs compared to hollow concrete blocks are supported by findings from: S. V. Gurupatham, C. Jayasinghe, and P. Perera, "Ranking of Walling Materials Using Eco-Efficiency for Tropical Climatic Conditions: A Survey-Based Approach," *Energy and Buildings* 253 (December 15, 2021).

cussed masonry types—hollow concrete blocks, CSEBs, and CEBs—as well as their associated costs are considered. In addition to the blocks, the calculations include all other materials that are part of the wall construction. For the concrete block construction, this includes reinforced concrete columns, lintels, and ring beams. In the CSEB and CEB types, conversely, the blocks themselves are load-bearing, eliminating the need for concrete columns but requiring lintels above doors and windows as well as ring beams at the transition to the roof. Furthermore, concrete block construction requires a surface finish with plaster and paint, which is counterproductive for CSEB construction. For CEB walls, however, since the blocks themselves do not contain cement, a protective weatherproofing layer on the outside is required. We have tested a bamboo cladding in our living laboratory with satisfactory results.

Any material requirements and costs of additional components that are identical for all three masonry types, such as foundation, roof, doors, or windows, were not taken into considered in this analysis. ●52

With costs of nearly 6,500 CFA francs per square meter of wall surface (approximately €9.80 per square meter), concrete block construction marks by far the most expensive option. In CSEB construction, costs are reduced by about 45 percent to around 3,500 CFA francs per square meter of wall surface (approximately €5.50 per square meter). The CEB type performs even better; omitting cement in the blocks halves their cost. Despite additional expenses for the bamboo weatherproofing, the total expenses for materials decrease by over 50 percent to around 3,000 CFA francs per square meter of wall surface (approximately €4.60 per square meter). However, depending on the local cost of labor, the additional layer required by CEBs can render them more expensive than CSEBs.

The comparison illustrates that it is not the prices of the blocks themselves, but the systems in which they are applied that drives their economic performances apart. A square meter of pure masonry made from concrete blocks incurs material costs of 2,310 CFA francs (€3.50), while the same surface made from CSEBs costs 2,094 CFA francs (€3.20). It is only when combined with the additional material requirements of each system that the costs significantly differentiate. For instance, plaster and paint alone increase the costs for concrete block construction by 20 percent. In contrast, the simplicity of earth-based masonry, consisting of fewer layers overall, minimizes material costs and simplifies construction processes.[52]

However, the conclusion must also entail the recognition that lintels and ring beams represent signifi-

	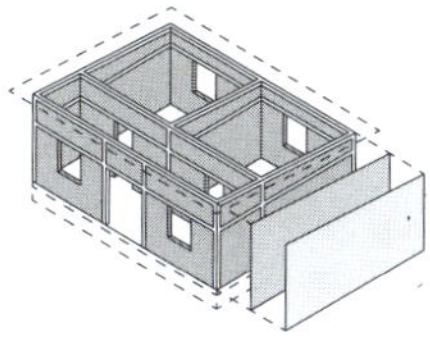	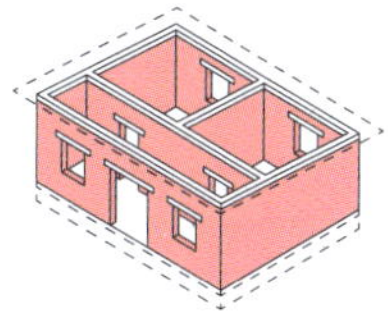	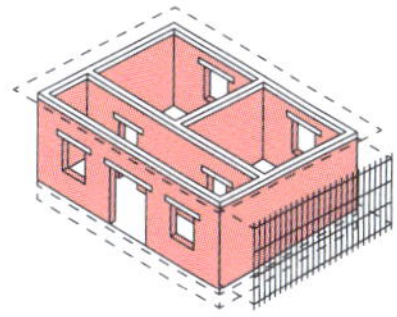
MODEL HOUSE	**CONCRETE BLOCK**	**CSEB**	**CEB**
Floor Space	48 m^2	48 m^2	48 m^2
Room Height	2.8–3.2 m	2.8–3.2 m	2.8–3.2 m
Masonry Units	≈ 1,125	≈ 4,350	≈ 4,350
MATERIAL REQUIREMENTS			
Masonry Blocks	9.36 m^3	22.34 m^3	22.34 m^3
Concrete Components	3.1 m^3	2.45 m^3	2.45 m^3
Reinforcing Steel Bars [Ø 6 mm]	0.21 m^3	0.10 m^3	0.10 m^3
Plaster [20 mm]	3.56 m^3	-	-
Paint	110 l	-	-
Bamboo	-	-	0.47 m^3
FINANCIAL COSTS [in CFA francs]			
Masonry Blocks	205,844	194,920	96,495
Concrete Components	69,080	51,700	51,700
Reinforcing Steel Bars [Ø 6 mm]	188,838	88,974	88,974
Plaster [20 mm]	78,417	-	-
Paint	32,080	-	-
Bamboo	-	-	46,535
Total	**574,259**	**335,594**	**283,704**
Costs / m^2 Wall Construction	**6,444**	**3,606**	**3,048**
Reduction Potential	-	**44%**	**52%**
ENVIRONMENTAL COSTS [in kg CO_2-eq. (A1–A3)]			
Masonry Blocks[a, b, c]	4,010	3,592	172
Concrete Components[b, c]	1,617	1,210	1,210
Reinforcing Steel Bars[d] [Ø 6 mm]	1,126	531	531
Plaster[b, c] [20 mm]	1,836	-	-
Paint[e]	223	-	-
Bamboo Façade[d, f]	-	-	100
Total	**9,620**	**5,333**	**2013**
Costs / m^2 Wall Construction	**108**	**57**	**22**
Reduction Potential	-	**47%**	**80%**

● 52 Material Cost and Environmental Impacts of Concrete Block-, CSEB-, and CEB-Model Houses ***(→ p. 134)***

cant factors in the economic and environmental costs of all types of wall construction. Due to the limited availability of timber in the region and the virtual absence of sawmills, it is not possible to forgo reinforced concrete ring beams in Mako, but an exploration of employing timber for such applications is encouraged in regions with sustainable access to wood-based building products. The only optimization possible for our work in Mako is currently the masonry arch, which can substitute the reinforced concrete lintels for wall openings.

Along with the ring beams, the foundations and ceilings are equally difficult to be fabricated from regenerative materials. Although Studio Suddo Neuve proposed an iteration for ceiling construction using load-bearing CSEBs, the demand for these blocks *(→ p. 84)* has been nonexistent. The reason for the lack of demand can be attributed to the format of the ceiling blocks and their associated construction sequence, which are not compatible with the prevailing system of concrete ceiling blocks. While both systems are based on the logic of reinforced concrete beams into which the blocks are inserted, the CSEBs require a more precise execution of the beams. This is extremely challenging in Mako due to the absence of accurate formworks and the necessary equipment, such as mobile cranes, to install the prefabricated beams on the construction site. As most of the current CSEB building projects are single-story structures, we have focused on masonry blocks but intend to explore ways to increase the use of ceiling blocks in the future.

Since 2023, Studio Suddo Neuve has been conducting its production operations at its own manufacturing site. Several reasons have contributed to the decision to transition from an initially mobile production to a fixed location. As outlined in the manual, the production process requires a considerable amount of space *(→ pp. 70–73)*. During on-site production, particularly when other construction activities were already underway, it was challenging to have an uninterrupted flow. Another factor prompting this transition was the desired separation of order placement and drying times of blocks. We noticed that customers preferred to commence with their construction shortly after inquiring about the bricks, maintaining a stock of blocks proved advantageous to fulfill orders quickly. This also allowed us to replenish inventory during regular production cycles rather than in spontaneous on-demand productions, which has proven to be also economically more viable.

We conduct our production operations in an open-air setting with a total area of 400 square meters. The plot sits on level ground, with material deliveries facilitated through a large gate. Positioned centrally is a paved platform where the blocks are pressed *(→ p. 66)*. Adjacent to this platform lies a small workshop building serving as an office and as tool storage. Water is provided by a newly constructed well. These elements lay the groundwork for production, with plans underway to further develop infrastructure for production optimization in the future. Moreover, the site is designated to host practical research. Projects like the living lab and other prototypes are envisioned to be developed on-site to advance work through practical experimentation. ●53

Due to outdoor operations, the annual production window is confined to the dry season (from

●53 NiokoBâti Earth Block Manufacturing Site

53 For the life cycle assessments we used data records from Ökobaudat, a building materials database by the German Federal Ministry of Housing, Urban Development and Construction.

November to May), with a break during the fasting month of Ramadan. Within this timeframe, three production series of approximately one month each (twenty working days) are scheduled, each yielding around 15,000 blocks. Prior to each production cycle, material organization takes place. Following the production, we oversee the curing and storage of the blocks. This form of operation allows us to employ two permanent staff members and engage an additional ten employees during production. Fully developed, the site is designed to achieve a production capacity of 45,000 blocks per year, equivalent to about ten of the typical single-story two-bedroom houses in Mako. More so than the pioneer demonstration building that initially sparked interest in CSEB construction in Mako, the production facility enables the replication and adaptation of our proposed architecture and enables us to work more cost-effectively.

The impact of introducing CSEB architecture to Mako can further be quantified using the tool of comparative LCA. As with the costs, this is best executed using the example of the model house, where the different blocks are considered within their respective building systems. If 45,000 CSEBs are substituting the equivalent of their concrete counterparts in the form of ten model houses, approximately 45 tons of carbon dioxide equivalents can be saved in Mako annually. If unstabilized CEBs were applied, the saving increases by a factor of 1.8 to over 80 tons of carbon dioxide equivalents (→ *p. 105* for a detailed breakdown of the comparative LCA).

Causing around a third of the total emissions for all three types, the assessment shows that lintels and ring anchors have a major influence on the overall balance. Additionally, the already poor performance of the concrete block version is reinforced in the assessments of the surface materials. While the cement-based plaster and the associated paint coating for a model house in concrete block construction emit around 2,000 kilograms of carbon dioxide equivalents, they are not required at all for CSEBs. The exterior bamboo cladding of the CEB walls even sequesters over 200 kilograms of carbon. As there are no specific datasets available for Mako, the generic datasets used herein operate with a degree of uncertainty.[53] For instance, materials such as sand and earth are attributed disproportionately long transportation distances, and the environmental costs of cement and steel are not aligned with national production standards. The high proportion of regional building materials for earth masonry, which require minimal or no production steps after extraction, would likely improve its ecological footprint and further differentiate it from the concrete alternative.

Voices: Cultivating Earth Blocks in Mako

A conversation with Issa Diallo, Alexander Duerr, and Micha Kretschmann

Founding members of Studio Suddo Neuve Issa Diallo, Alexander Duerr, and Micha Kretschmann reflect on their work of recent years. Starting with a review of the pioneer demonstration building of 2020, they look back on the genesis of the collective and the earth-block production and application. Looking to the future, they discuss practical steps to improve the establishment of their manufactory as a driver for the regenerative urbanization of Mako. The edited transcript is a compilation of a series of conversations.

Micha Kretschmann Following an initial two years of research and experimentation, we finished the construction of our demonstration building, in 2020. In retrospect, what do you recall of the building's completion, how has it changed since then?

Issa Diallo We were incredibly proud when the building was completed in April 2020. With the COVID-19 pandemic beginning to restrict life and work, and our team members drained from months of research, manufacturing, and construction; it was a tremendous relief to see our building stand strong and to receive compliments and interest from all sides. Beyond the structure itself, the project has shaped us as a team, and we became the first and only player associated with modern earth construction in the region. Even beyond that, it was the first time a building really exhibited innovation.

Alexander Duerr Programmatically, I would say the building is a success. The shop on the ground floor is vibrant and the apartment with the large rooftop terrace quickly found tenants. The technical installations for electricity and water are also functioning well. After the first rainy season in the summer of 2020, we were happy to see that the building had withstood the weathering. However, it did sustain some damages. Algae growth became a problem, and the top row of blocks of the parapet suffered under the constant rain exposure, especially because it was not angled. As a first measure, we covered the masonry parapet with sheet metal and re-rendered the façades, this time with a bit more cement in our mortar. Our observation is that this issue is closely tied to the architectural style of the building. The design was to compete with the neighboring structures along the road in its aesthetics. In hindsight, we would not recommend constructing such monolithic structures with flat roofs, masonry parapets, and large, unprotected façades. We had also underestimated the drainage volume of the flat roofs and terraces, and are currently working on installing additional drainage outlets. ●54

MK While the reworking of our first demonstration building remains a constant work in progress, a significant aspect of the revision process has involved applying the newly gained knowledge to other projects. For example, in contrast to our pioneer building, following projects included building pitched roofs or roofs with an overhang. Altering our recipe and improving quality control measures, we have significantly improved the quality of our earth blocks; nowadays they are much more weather-resistant than those we used in our first building. What kind of feedback do you get from clients that have built with our blocks?

ID All throughout the follow-up projects we received very positive feedback, and the increasing number of completed projects is helping to dismantle existing prejudices against earth-based construction. Especially, regarding the interior temperatures, all our clients are reporting the high comfort of the buildings during the dry season. Many people want to build smaller buildings from earth blocks for their elderly parents now, to increase their comfort.

However, we have not yet achieved the same standing as our concrete competitors, and this is not only because of their materiality but also due to our mode of operation. It appears that a lot of people prefer to purchase raw materials and negotiate production costs of concrete blocks with their trusted brickmakers over buying our prefabricated product at a fixed price. Especially because the CSEBs only become cheaper through the follow-up costs of the construction. As people can rarely finance an entire project in advance, the concrete blocks give them a maximum of flexibility in terms of spreading out investment costs for resources and labor. This is a general phenomenon in Mako, extending beyond the field of construction. Nonetheless, with more and more wage labor and even a bank in Mako now, loans have become more accessible and the reliable purchase of a finished product more tangible and attractive to most people.

MK Another factor challenging our model is the deviation from the conventional practice in project design, typically handled by the client and their mason. Substituting concrete blocks with CSEBs disrupts this model, requiring us to extend our services beyond block production to include design consultancy and project supervision. How do you see this playing out?

AD Rather challenging. The most successful projects are those where we are involved from start to finish—as designers, producers of the blocks, and even as construction supervisors, at least until the masonry is completed. Simply put, delivering a truckload of blocks to a client seldomly works in Mako's current building economy. But as more masons become familiar with the material, less project support is required.

ID We also had to learn through experience that project support must be balanced even when trying to promote our material. Some of the earlier cases were particularly frustrating: Once, we designed what could have become our largest project, a development comprising three shops in the basement and apartments on top, likely three times the size of previous projects. In collaboration with the interested builder, we developed the design and fully detailed the project including expected costs and the number of blocks required. After a few weeks of not hearing back from the client, we were surprised to see the construction commencing without a placed order for bricks. When the building was finished it became clear that they had used our plans and details but built it from concrete blocks, without compensating us for any of our work.

AD Although the projects that we accompany more thoroughly have a higher quality in their execution, we find it challenging in our current setup to offer adequate support beyond the production of high-quality blocks. As a work-around, we have initiated discussions with Maçon Beifall, a renowned mason in Mako who has previously worked with CSEBs. In Mako, he is responsible for almost all projects involving multistory construction. Due to the high volume of projects, he is overwhelmed with organizing the production of concrete blocks for his projects. A long-term collaboration with Maçon Beifall could increase the confidence in our earth-based products due to his professionalism in the execution, and we could focus on our core competency of handling the value chains for earth-block production.

MK This takes us to our production facility that we inaugurated in 2023 to produce blocks at a centralized location in Mako. The facility allows us to produce 45,000 blocks per dry season and with the prospects of collaborations like the one with Maçon Beifall, the demand will continue to increase. Do you think that we can handle a steady demand for our blocks?

ID Absolutely! The production yard is a game changer. The process is much more efficient. When we were operating as a mobile production, we struggled to produce 500 blocks a day due constantly changing circumstances of the production. On our site, we can produce 750, maybe even 800 blocks. This makes the enterprise more economically viable, and it's also more enjoyable when things are running smoothly, and you don't start the day with surprises. Our quality control indicators, such as compressive strength and dimensional accuracy, have improved since we started production at our site. Additionally, we have advantages in logistics. We can stock our raw materials in large quantities, and drying the blocks is no longer as challenging since we are not spatially constrained and don't need to level the ground before stacking. However, as of today, everything we do is done manually. Only recently, we installed a solar pump for our well, which is our first electrical equipment. Particularly, breaking and sieving the soil is disproportionately exhausting and slow. We are considering solving this by introducing a motorized crusher. This would be a significant gain and might even increase our output and profitability. We also envision storing the raw materials (earth, sand, cement) in bulk storages in paved and partially covered spaces to streamline logistics at the site.

AD Another benefit of constructing our own manufacturing site was using it as a full-scale prototype for improved construction methods. For instance, we have long thought about a hybrid roof structure: integrating a straw-loam infill within a timber-bamboo framework and topped with an air-vented metal roof can effectively mitigate the intense heat of Mako and perform even better than the concrete ceilings. However, convincing clients to adopt this design without a tangible example has been challenging. Now, with the completion of our workshop building, in which we pioneered this structure, we are confident that it will soon be replicated in other projects. ●55

MK The jobs in the gold mine and the resulting higher purchasing power of the region are an important factor for the current urbanization activity in Mako. However, with the expected depletion of gold at the current extraction site, major changes are expected to affect the community. Do you think our earth-block production is resilient enough eventually face this change?

ID From my perspective, gold initially fueled our urbanization, but it wasn't the only driver. The opening of a secondary school, the connection to the national road, the installation of an electricity grid, and many other reasons have contributed to these developments. As a result, today much of Mako's life revolves around a service-based economy and I believe we've reached a scale where the urbanization is self-sustaining and will continue in spite of the decreasing significance of the mining sector. In that sense, I am also confident that the demand for earth blocks will be sustained.

Regarding resilience, I'd like to highlight two factors, which are less related to the gold mine and more to our ties to international markets. Firstly, our expenses primarily consist of labor costs. Providing job opportunities and circulating money

●55 Construction of a Roofing Detail for Our Workshop Building

●56 Members of Studio Suddo Nouvo during the Construction of the Living Lab

within our local economy, the blocks have a certain political power. Clients have started to see that. They realize that the money that they would otherwise spend on cement now goes into the pockets of the young men working on our production site. Family and community is still very important here, if people can support each other like this, they will. Secondly, in Mako, cement and steel are frequently out of stock. Not only during the pandemic but whenever the global market is stressed, we face shortages. Suddenly, a bag of cement costs 6,000 CFA francs (€9.11) instead of 4,500 CFA francs (€6.83) or is not available at all. Focusing on local resources has shielded us from these shortages to a significant extent.

AD This is why it has become increasingly important for us to complement the earth blocks with other nature-based and locally-available materials. We have found that other traditional building materials, such as bamboo and typha, can also be included into building assemblies that respond to the current demand for architecture in Mako. It seems to me that the more we transition toward a regional building culture, the less stress we invite to our everyday lives. ●56●57

1 LIVING LAB
2 PILOT BUILDING
3 HENHOUSE
4 ONE-ROOM HOUSING UNIT
5 BUILDING EXTENSION
6 CORNER STORE
7 BUNGALOW RESIDENCE
8 CLASSROOM
9 ENCLOSING WALL
10 WORKSHOP BUILDING

● 57 Overview: Realized CSEB Structures in Mako, Senegal

Forecast

Beyond Blocks

The momentum and haste of Mako's urbanization came with both uncertainty and openness that made it plausible to embark on this intervention—an intervention to envision, explore, and materialize a nature-based thread that weaves itself into the growing urban fabric. In our efforts to explore ways of returning to earth in Mako, we challenge prevailing norms, confirm and refute known merits of earth and concrete alike, and ultimately find ourselves short on many fronts.

Although the appearance of our demonstration buildings suggests a viability of transitioning back to earth, the earthen walls of the multistory buildings are deceiving. The picture-perfect façades hide the concrete foundations, the rebars in the ring beams, and most importantly the 6-percent cement in the CSEBs themselves. We do not wish to undermine their potential in reducing the carbon footprint of the built environment. After all, CSEBs reduce emissions by over 40 percent compared to concrete blocks. However, upon closer examination, it becomes evident that our proposed CSEB typologies rely heavily on significant quantities of cement and steel, thereby perpetuating a dependence on carbon-intensive, fossil-based supply chains. Or at least they do not manage to escape it.

In assessing materials beyond the usual parameters of price, performance, and aesthetics to also encompass the before- and afterlife of architectural artefacts along with the socioeconomic conditions in which they are engendered, we had to recognize that infrastructural and skill gaps as well as the unavailability of materials continuously pushed us back toward the conventional. An expanded notion of beauty that includes sites of material extraction, the needs of inhabitants, and the end-of-life reintegration of materials into natural cycles, remains the utopian vision. However, seven years of work in and with Mako and its surrounding ecosystems of bio- and geo-based resources offer a starting point to develop post-fossil alternatives to the pervasive spread of concrete.

In hindsight, it was not our expertise, but rather the constant practical experimentation, refinement, and adaptation that allowed us to develop a competency to co-create Mako's urban fabric. Rather than perfecting the architecture on paper, we continue to test and prototype real-use structures, sacrificing maximum environmental sustainability for safety and replicability but deriving learnings from each built building. Documented, our work shows this continuous evolution driven by different factors at different times. Each building iteration is an improvement that produces new knowledge and new questions. Thus, the constructed references become outdated in respect to our knowledge from the moment of their completion and enable us to further improve in forthcoming projects.

The approach of simply exchanging one type of block for another seems naïve to us today. While it served as a starting point, it lacks the complexity necessary to address all potential areas for improving building typologies toward environmental sustainability and user friendliness. Replacing a concrete block with a stabilized compressed earth block is the most elementary part of the intervention; however, this sustainable transformation of masonry construction is complicated by the necessity to create an economically competitive value chain for the production of CSEBs and to convince builders of the material's qualities despite preexisting prejudices against earth architecture. In this process, the CSEB architecture remains for us a transitory element in the transformation back to earth. As new insights, which we experience day by day, shape our conception of earth blocks and their capabilities, we can no longer confidently propagate their stabilized version as our final proposal for a regenerative built environment.

When the block is considered within its system of construction, and its performance and added value are measured in three-dimensional space, additional levers emerge that more comprehensively address the goal of regenerative construction methods. Here, the leap from individual blocks to a comprehensive system has revealed that a regenerative urbanization cannot be carried by a singular product; rather, it demands a transformation of the entire material culture of local construction. While earth blocks may hold a pivotal position in the emerging urban fabric, other threads will need to emerge and contribute to the formation. Our buildings show that the careful alteration, subtraction, and addition of building components can improve their performance environmentally and practically. Thereby, the maintenance of the earth architecture is the most insightful part of the architectural process. Through the continuous monitoring of the buildings we built, we gather valuable learnings. While some components proved to have the intended effect, others failed and were replaced. Seeing the structures age is now giving us the confidence to increasingly use CEBs for applicable purposes. Particularly, the approach of combining CSEBs and CEBs and using the bio-based materials bamboo and typha grass harbors significant potential that we envision merging into promising components and structures as we further develop the necessary skills and value chains. ●**58**

Earthbound Futures

Our process shows that the re-entanglement with the natural environment is a much slower process than the disconnection triggered by the integration into extractive economic systems. Replacing earth and bamboo with concrete and steel comes easier than reversing this trend. Much more than the building materials, it is these creative processes of conceiving a context-specific architecture and continuously adapting it to respond to the environment and its users that we see as our intervention in Mako today. The interventional framing of the work allowed for the unusual cooperation between masons, welders, carpenters, students, and architects to follow need and not financial interest and to find architectural solutions for a region that, due to meager capital means, is often overlooked.

We see this intervention now, with the publication of this manual, as concluded and are intrigued to observe the future adaptation and application in Mako's progression from village to town.

With *Back to Earth*, we hope to extend the impact of our work beyond the borders of Senegal's Kedougou region and propagate the rediscovery of earth as a building material as one possible solution to reduce the environmental impact of building. Re-entangling with the Earth's systems demands careful consideration of the impacts of our actions and a shift toward prioritizing long-term objectives over immediate gains, within

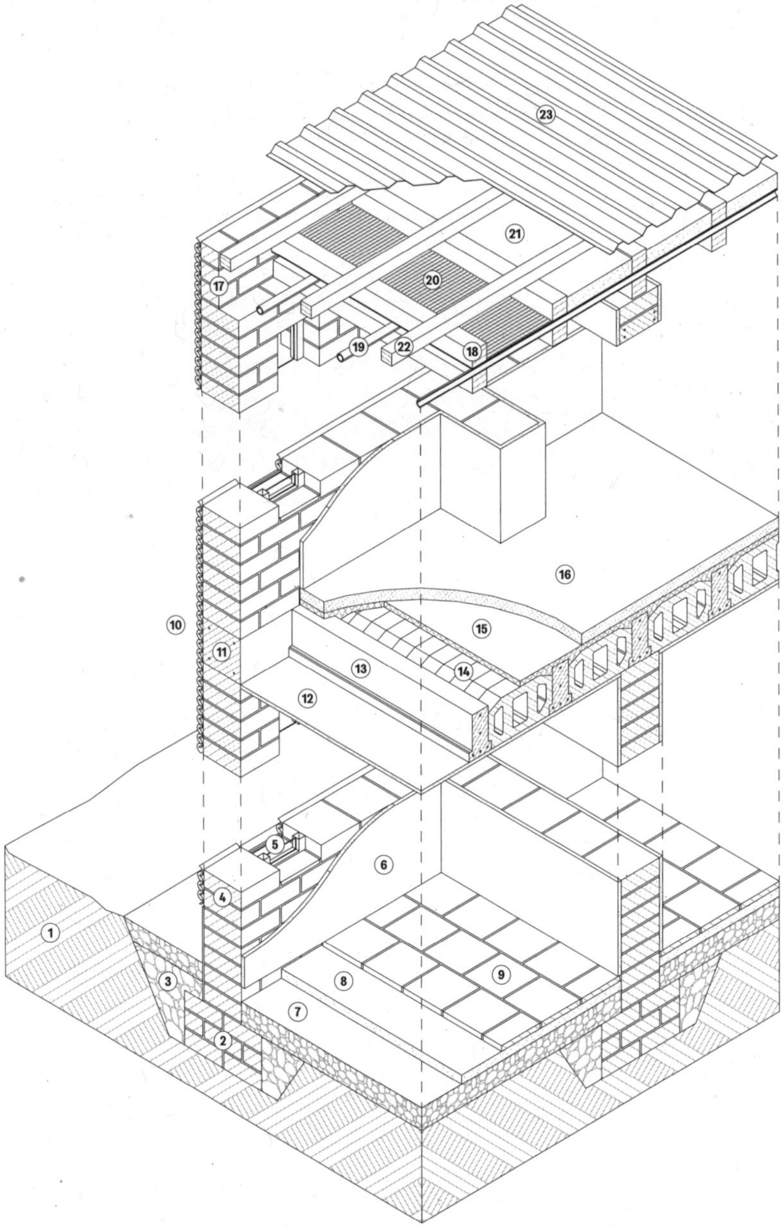

1. NATURAL SOIL
2. CSEB MASONRY FOUNDATION
3. GRAVEL DRAINAGE
4. CEB MASONRY
5. STEELFRAME WINDOW
6. EARTH PLASTER
7. LATERITE GRAVEL LAYER
8. SANDBED
9. SEALED CSEB-TILES
10. BAMBOO CLADDING
11. REINFORCED CONCRETE BEAM
12. CLAY PLASTER
13. REINFORCED CONCRETE BEAM
14. CEILING BLOCK
15. TYPHA BOARD
16. RAMMED EARTH TERRAZZO
17. CSEB MASONRY
18. DOUBLED TIMBER BEAM
19. BAMBOO CANE
20. BAMBOO MAT
21. STRAW-EARTH FILLING
22. SLOPED TIMBER BEAM
23. SHEET METAL

58 Fictional Design of an Optimized Earth Block Structure

54 Mazen Bouri, "Build Capacity to Expand Access for All to Housing Finance in West Africa," *World Bank Blogs,* November 2023, https://blogs.worldbank.org/en/africacan/build-capacity-expand-access-all-housing-finance-west-africa, last accessed September 23, 2024.

55 Hannah Ritchie, Max Roser, and Pablo Rosado, "Energy," *Our World in Data*, October 27, 2022, https://ourworldindata.org/co2/country/senegal, last accessed July 8, 2024.

a contextually tailored approach to effecting change. Imagining a reorientation of the building sector driven by the local availability of materials and the specificities of climates, a (re)-diversification of architecture emerges in which earth can play a significant role, in which we become earthbound again. Addressing the complexities that come with a plurality of regionally specific futures within globally interconnected systems represents a challenge for science and practice, yet it is essential for securing a future of our planet.

The past seven years were the starting point for this process in Mako. As it is not an already-established urban conglomerate, Mako has allowed for the early integration of alternative materials into the urbanization process. Nonetheless, our work shows that the reintroduction of earth to local building cultures does not only demand earth to become competitive with conventional materials; rather it recalibrates the expectations toward architecture: "Faster, higher, stronger" can no longer serve as the guiding principle; instead, architecture needs to be defined by the availability of local resources and the harmonization of form with the natural capabilities of building materials. Along with the development of other regenerative building materials and techniques to complement earth blocks, it is this shift in building ethos that will enable the unstabilized version of earth blocks to succeed.

Nonetheless, our work shows that the impact CSEBs and ultimately CEBs can have on the reduction of the environmental costs of construction is significant. Recalling the starting point of our endeavor, which looked at current building patterns in the region, we argue that the replacement of concrete blocks with CSEBs and CEBs is viable and can constitute a major pillar of regenerative construction in the West African region. Current projections suggest a total housing deficit of 3.5 million units in the region, creating a building demand of 250,000 units per annum to adequately respond to population growth and urbanization.[54] If all these houses were to be built from CSEBs, one million fewer tons of carbon dioxide would be emitted annually when compared to the predicted emissions of concrete blocks, equating to almost 10 percent of Senegal's total annual carbon dioxide emissions.[55] If they were to be built from CEBs, 1.9 million fewer tons of carbon dioxide would be emitted annually. This rift will only be possible if earth blocks are produced both in a decentralized way and cost effectively to outcompete concrete; an initial attempt for this strategy is laid out in this book.

We sought innovation in a place that had accepted its concrete fate and is hence representative for many places around the world. Our vision for an

● 59 Street View of Living Lab

urbanization without depletion draws attention to the possibility for a more sustainable architecture and offers a tangible starting point as an intervention that can be activated in built environments around the globe in its methodology as well as in its materiality. Certainly, our work also has its imperfections and leaves room for improvement. In this manual we try to reflect the state of our knowledge and allow insight into its origins, weak points, and prospective improvements. In today's circumstances the combination of technical innovation, environmental consciousness, and social responsibility is often a triage. As Studio Suddo Neuve we argue that it is time to take practical measures toward the move back into planetary boundaries. By writing this manual, we hope to set a precedent for this transformation and ease the process for those who want to effect change in other places. We are trying to avert the impending crisis and hope you will join us in this effort. ●59

Glossary

Bauhaus Earth
Bauhaus Earth is an interdisciplinary and international think-and-make tank based in Berlin, Germany. The non-profit organization is dedicated to the regenerative transformation of the built environment. Founded in 2019 by climate scientist Hans Joachim "John" Schellnhuber, today Bauhaus Earth brings together experts from the fields of science, architecture and planning, governance, and industry.

Cement
Mixed with the aggregates sand and gravel, cement is the binding agent in concrete. The manufacturing of cement requires high levels of primary energy and is a significant source of the building industry's greenhouse gas emissions and construction and demolition waste.

Compressed earth blocks
Compressed earth blocks (CEBs) are masonry blocks made from earth. The only binder in CEBs is clay, making them one-hundred-percent recyclable and minimizing their carbon footprint, as firing is not required. CEBs differ from adobe blocks in that they are highly compacted, resulting in improved compressive strength and water resistance. High-quality CEBs can be used as structural elements but generally need to be constructively protected from moisture, such as rain and rising damp.

Compressed stabilized earth blocks
Compressed stabilized earth blocks (CSEBs) are a kind of masonry block based on earth, with cement as an additional stabilizer. In comparison to concrete blocks, they benefit from reduced financial and environmental costs, while sustaining high compressive strengths and water resistance. They are most commonly used for monolithic masonry construction in architecture projects around the world.

Curing
Curing of both concrete blocks and CSEBs describes the maintenance of adequate moisture and temperature conditions for the hydraulic binding of the cement to take place. By preventing the loss of water through evaporation, properly cured materials are of higher quality.

French (language)
A trace of colonial heritage, French is the official language of twenty-seven countries; among them is Senegal. Liberated from French colonial rule in 1960, today only a small part of the population speaks French.

Fula
The Fula (also referred to as Fulani or Fulbe) people are an ethnic group primarily found in the Sahara and Sahel zone in West Africa. An estimate of 25 to 40 million Fula live across the region, around one third of the population is pastoralist, making them the largest nomadic pastoral community globally. Despite their spread in the West African region, the Fula share a common language (Pulaar), history, and culture.

International Style
A modernist architectural style with its roots in the early twentieth century. With an industrial, pragmatic, and pure language of form and color, its universalist approach quickly spread around the world.

Intervention
Intervention is defined as a conscious act of becoming involved with the intention of altering the outcome. In our work we use the term to describe our interference with the universalization of concrete block architecture in the West African urbanization process.

Life cycle assessment (LCA)
The process of assessing the environmental costs that a particular product, such as a building material, has over the course of its

life. Differentiated into the stages of production, installation, use, and end-of-life processing, the analyses allow for the identification of optimization potentials to minimize the environmental impact of the product as well as to inform a choice between competing products.

Living lab
A full-scale structure of a research element that is subjected to real stresses and observed over time. Lessons learned from living labs are used to validate theoretical or laboratory research results. An example of this can be a demonstration component or building that uses innovative building materials and techniques.

Manual
Guided instructions on a specific topic. Characterized by detailed insights into a case study, manuals invite replication.

NiokoBâti
A Mako-based company for earth building and one of the two main collaborators of Studio Suddo Neuve.

Planetary boundaries
A term used to recall the natural limits of the Earth system. Recognizing the impact of human activity as a key factor in the increasingly critical, global climate crisis, operating within planetary boundaries implies a regenerative governance that preserves resources, landscapes, and ultimately ecosystems on a global scale.

Project Mako e.V.
A non-profit architecture association from Germany and one of two main collaborators of Studio Suddo Neuve.

Pulaar
One of the seven national languages of Senegal. Spoken primarily by the Fula and Toucouleur people, Pulaar is the most widely spoken language in Mako.

Re-entangle
After decades of artificial separation of humans and nature, re-entangling describes the effort of revive the inherent relationship and interdependence of human settlements and their natural surroundings. This process involves an interdisciplinary effort. In the building industry, the focus lies on the transformation of extractive and fossil-based material cultures to more regenerative and circular solutions.

Slaking
Slaking is the process of allowing moist earth to rest for up to forty-eight hours to fully mobilize the clay platelets. As a result, earth blocks made from slaked earth have higher compressive strength than those made immediately after wetting.

Soil/earth
Soil, sometimes referred to as earth, is part of the outermost layer of Earth's crust. It consists of loose minerals that are mixed with organic and living matter, as well as gases and liquids. In the construction context, the building material soil/earth most often describes a homogeneous, loamy material, free of organic matter, that can be used for the production of earth blocks (CEBs and CSEBs), walls, renders, and paints.

Vernacular architecture
Vernacular architecture refers to buildings built with locally available materials and techniques specific to the culture of a place. Contemporary architectural discourse often contrasts newer styles, such as the International Style, with the vernacular in an effort to identify pathways for a revitalized, pluralistic, and climate-adaptive practice.

West Africa
West Africa refers to the western part of the African continent, located south of the Sahara and north of the equator. Following countries are commonly included when describing the region: Benin, Burkina Faso, Cabo Verde, Ivory Coast, Gambia, Ghana, Guinea, Guinea-Bissau, Liberia, Mali, Mauritania, Niger, Nigeria, Saint Helena, Senegal, Sierra Leone, and Togo.

Bibliography

Adam, E.A., and A.R.A. Agib. *Compressed Stabilised Earth Block Manufacture in Sudan* (Paris: UNESCO, July 2001).
→ https://unesdoc.unesco.org/ark:/48223/pf0000128236. Accessed September 23, 2024.

African Development Bank. " African Development Bank Statistical Data Portal." December 2023.
→ https://dataportal.opendataforafrica.org/. Accessed July 8, 2024.

Agence Française de Développement. "Cement, Confronting Ecological Responsibility and Economic Imperatives" May 2011.
→ https://www.proparco.fr/en/ressources/cement-confronting-ecological-responsibility-and-economic-imperatives. Accessed September 23, 2024.

Boubekeur, Sid, Vincent Rigassi, Ali Mesbah, Jean-Claude Morel, Hugo Houben, and Wilfredo Carazas. *Compressed Earth Blocks: Testing Procedures*. Brussels: CDE, 2000.
→ https://craterre.hypotheses.org/4003. Accessed September 23, 2024.

Bouchard-Huzard, Louis. *Traité des constructions rurales et de leur disposition*. Paris: Mme. V. Bouchard-Huzard, 1869.
→ http://archive.org/details/traitedesconstru02bouc. Accessed September 23, 2024.

Bouri, Mazen. "Build Capacity to Expand Access for All to Housing Finance in West Africa." *World Bank Blogs,* November 2023.
→ https://blogs.worldbank.org/en/africacan/build-capacity-expand-access-all-housing-finance-west-africa. Accessed September 23, 2024.

Brinkmann, Maximilian, and Philipp Wiehle. "Correlation between Relative Humidity and the Strength and Deformation Characteristics of Unstabilised Earth Masonry." *Construction and Building Materials* 366 (February 2023).
→ https://doi.org/10.1016/j.conbuildmat.2022.130048.

Bureau of Indian Standards. *IS 1725: 2023: Stabilized Soil Blocks Used in General Building Construction Specification*, New Delhi, March 2023
→ http://archive.org/details/gov.in.is.1725.2023. Accessed September 23, 2024.

Byiers, Bruce, Karim Karaki, and Jan Vanheukelom. "Regional Markets, Politics and Value Chains: The Case of West African Cement." *European Centre for Development Policy Management*, no. 216 (September 2017).

Cassiman, Ann, ed. *Architectures of Belonging: Inhabiting Worlds in Rural West Africa*. Antwerp: BAI Pub, 2011.

Choplin, Armelle. "Cementing Africa: Cement Flows and City-Making along the West African Corridor (Accra, Lomé, Cotonou, Lagos)." *Urban Studies* 57, no. 9 (July 2020): 1977–93.
→ https://doi.org/10.1177/0042098019851949.

Crawford, Elisabeth T. *Arrhenius: From Ionic Theory to the Greenhouse Effect*. Uppsala Studies in History of Science, vol. 23. Canton, MA: Science History Publications/USA, 1996

Darman, Japhet Taypondou, Jules Hermann Keyangue Tchouata, Gilbert François Ngôn Ngôn, François Ngapgue, Bachirou Lindou Ngakoupain, and Yannick Tchedele Langollo. "Evaluation of Lateritic Soils of Mbé for Use as Compressed Earth Bricks (CEB)." *Heliyon* 8, no. 8 (August 2022).
→ https://doi.org/10.1016/j.heliyon.2022.e10147.

Dethier, Jean, Heinrich Klotz, and Karl Heinz Striedter. *Lehmarchitektur: Die Zukunft einer vergessenen Bautradition.* Munich: Prestel Verlag, 1982.

Deutsches Institut für Normung, ed. DIN 18940:2022-10, *Load-Bearing Earth Block Masonry: Construction, Design and Execution.* Berlin: Beuth Verlag, 2022.
→ https://doi.org/10.31030/3382418.

Deutsches Institut für Normung, ed. DIN 18945:2018-12, *Earth Blocks Requirements, Test and Labelling.* Berlin: Beuth Verlag, 2018.
→ https://doi.org/10.31030/2897113.

Deutsches Institut für Normung, ed. DIN 18946:2018-12, *Earth Masonry Mortar. Requirements, Test and Labelling.* Berlin: Beuth Verlag, 2018.
→ https://doi.org/10.31030/2897114.

Elhacham, Emily, Liad Ben-Uri, Jonathan Grozovski, Yinon M. Bar-On, and Ron Milo. "Global Human-Made Mass Exceeds All Living Biomass." *Nature* 588, no. 7838 (December 2020): 442–44.
→ https://doi.org/10.1038/s41586-020-3010-5.

FAOSTAT Land, Inputs and Sustainability. "Climate Change Indicators; Temperature Change on Land." Rome, 2024.
→ http://www.fao.org/faostat/en/#data/ET. Accessed July 8, 2024.

Fayemiwo, Moshood Ademola, and Margie Marie Neal. *Aliko Mohammad Dangote: The Biography of the Richest Black Person in the World*. Houston, TX: Strategic Book Publishing and Rights Co, 2013.

Global Alliance for Buildings and Construction, International Energy Agency and the United Nations Environment Programme. "Global Status Report for Buildings and Construction 201—Analysis," December 11, 2019.
→ https://www.iea.org/reports/global-status-report-for-buildings-and-construction-2019. Accessed July 8, 2024.

Guihéneuf, Simon, Damien Rangeard, and Arnaud Perrot. "Cast, Compaction, Vibro-Compaction or Extrusion: Processing Methods for Optimizing the Mechanical Strength of Raw Earth-Based Materials," *Academic Journal of Civil Engineering* 37, no. 2, special issue. 3rd International Conference on Bio-Based Building Materials, Belfast, 2019 (2019): 156–63.

Gurupatham, S. V., C. Jayasinghe, and P. Perera. "Ranking of Walling Materials Using Eco-Efficiency for Tropical Climatic Conditions: A Survey-Based Approach." *Energy and Buildings* 253 (December 15, 2021).
→ https://doi.org/10.1016/j.enbuild.2021.111503.

Habert, Guillaume, Martin Röck, Karl Steininger, Antonin Lupisek, Harpa Birgisdottir, Harald Desing, Chanjief Chandrakumar, Francesco Pittau, Alexander Passer, Ronald Rovers, Katarina Slavkovic, Alexander Hollberg, Endrit Hoxha, Thomas Jusselme, Emilie Nault, Karen Allacker, and Thomas Lützkendorf. "Carbon Budgets for Buildings: Harmonising Temporal, Spatial and Sectoral Dimensions." *Buildings & Cities* 1, no. 1 (July 1, 2020).
→ https://doi.org/10.5334/bc.47.

Hermbstaedt, Sigismund Friedrich. *Bulletin des Neuesten und Wissenswürdigsten aus der Naturwissenschaft, so wie den Künsten, Manufakturen, technischen Gewerben der Landwirtschaft und der bürgerlichen Haushaltung*. Amelang, 1813.

Herz, Manuel, Ingrid Schröder, Hanz Focketyn, and Julia Jamrozik, eds. *African Modernism: The Architecture of Independence: Ghana, Senegal, Côte d'Ivoire, Kenya, Zambia*. Zurich: Park Books, 2015.

Houben, Hugo, and Hubert Guillaud. *Earth Construction: A Comprehensive Guide*. Intermediate Technology Publications, 1994.

IMARC Group. "Cement Market Report by Type, End Use, and Region (2024–2032)." (2023) → https://www.imarcgroup.com/cement-manufacturing-plant. Accessed June 12, 2024.

IMARC Group. "West Africa Cement Market Report by Type, End Use, and Country 2024–2032)," (2023) → https://www.imarcgroup.com/west-africa-cement-market. Accessed June 12, 2024.

International Energy Agency. *Energy Technology Perspectives 2016: Towards Sustainable Urban Energy Systems*. Paris, 2016. → https://www.iea.org/reports/energy-technology-perspectives-2016. Accessed July 8, 2024.

Iweriebor, Ehiedu E. G. *Dangote and Pan-Africa Economic Transformation: The Revolutionary Impact*. Bodija, Ibadan: Bookbuilders-Editions Africa, 2018.

Karkour, Selim, Safa Rachid, Mariem Maaoui, Zih-Ee Lin, and Norihiro Itsubo. "Status of Life Cycle Assessment (LCA) in Africa." *Environments* 8 (February 5, 2021): 10. → https://doi.org/10.3390/environments8020010.

Liu, Hengfeng, Jixiong Zhang, Baiyi Li, Nan Zhou, Xin Xiao, Meng Li, and Cunli Zhu. "Environmental Behavior of Construction and Demolition Waste as Recycled Aggregates for Backfilling in Mines: Leaching Toxicity and Surface Subsidence Studies." *Journal of Hazardous Materials* 389 (May 5, 2020). → https://doi.org/10.1016/j.jhazmat.2019.121870.

Lokko, Mae-ling, Frederick Wireko Manu, Nzinga Mboup, Mohamed Aly Etman, Marco Raugei, Ibrahim Niang, Kingdom Ametepe, and Rosemary Sarfo-Mensah. "Comparing the Whole Life Cycle Carbon Impact of Conventional and Biogenic Building Materials across Major Residential Typologies in Ghana and Senegal." *Sustainable Cities and Society* 106 (July 2024). → https://doi.org/10.1016/j.scs.2024.105332.

Mango-Itulamya, Lavie A., Frédéric Collin, Pascal Pilate, Fabienne Courtejoie, and Nathalie Fagel. "Evaluation of Belgian Clays for Manufacturing Compressed Earth Blocks." *Geologica Belgica* 22, no. 3–4 (December 15, 2019): 139–48. → https://doi.org/10.20341/gb.2019.002.

Marsh, Alastair T. M., and Yask Kulshreshtha. "The State of Earthen Housing Worldwide: How Development Affects Attitudes and Adoption." *Building Research & Information* 50, no. 5 (July 4, 2022): 485–501. → https://doi.org/10.1080/09613218.2021.1953369.

Minke, Gernot. *Building with Earth: Design and Technology of a Sustainable Architecture*. Basel, Boston: Birkhäuser, 2006.

Moussa, Hassane Seini, Philbert Nshimiyimana, Césaire Hema, Ousmane Zoungrana, Adamah Messan, and Luc Courard. "Comparative Study of Thermal Comfort Induced from Masonry Made of Stabilized Compressed Earth Block vs Conventional Cementitious Material." *Journal of Minerals and Materials Characterization and Engineering* 7, no. 6 (2019): 385–403. → https://doi.org/10.4236/jmmce.2019.76026.

OECD and Sahel and West Africa Club. *Africa's Urbanisation Dynamics 2020: Africapolis, Mapping a New Urban Geography*. West African Studies. OECD, 2020. → https://doi.org/10.1787/b6bccb81-en.

Padfield, Tim. "The Role of Absorbent Materials in Moderating Changes of Relative Humidity." PhD diss., The Technical University of Denmark, 1998.

Petrović, Emina Kristina, and Caroline Ann Thomas. "Global Patterns in Construction and Demolition Waste (C&DW) Research: A Bibliometric Analysis Using VOSviewer." *Sustainability* 16, no. 4 (January 2024). → https://doi.org/10.3390/su16041561.

Prussin, Labelle. "The Anthropology of Architecture and the Architecture of Anthropology." In *Architectures of Belonging: Inhabiting Worlds in Rural West Africa*, edited by Ann Cassiman. Antwerp: BAI Pub, 2011.

Purchase, Callun Keith, Dhafer Manna Al Zulayq, Bio Talakatoa O'Brien, Matthew Joseph Kowalewski, Aydin Berenjian, Amir Hossein Tarighaleslami, and Mostafa Seifan. "Circular Economy of Construction and Demolition Waste: A Literature Review on Lessons, Challenges, and Benefits." *Materials* 15, no. 1 (December 23, 2021): 76. → https://doi.org/10.3390/ma15010076.

Reddy, B. V. Venkatarama. *Compressed Earth Block and Rammed Earth Structures*. Springer Transactions in Civil and Environmental Engineering Ser. Singapore: Springer Singapore Pte. Limited, 2022.

Rigassi, Vincent, and CRATerre-EAG. *Compressed Earth Blocks: Volume 1. Manual of Production*. Braunschweig: Vieweg, 1995.

Ritchie, Hannah, Max Roser, and Pablo Rosado. "Energy." *Our World in Data*, October 27, 2022. → https://ourworldindata.org/co2/country/senegal. Accessed July 8, 2024.

Salman, Maha. "Sustainability and Vernacular Architecture: Rethinking What Identity Is." In *Urban and Architectural Heritage Conservation within Sustainability*, edited by Kabila Hmood. IntechOpen, 2019. → https://doi.org/10.5772/intechopen.82025.

Smith, S M, O Geden, M J Gidden, W F Lamb, G F Nemet, J C Minx, H Buck, et al. "The State of Carbon Dioxide Removal—2nd Edition." The State of Carbon Dioxide Removal, 2024. → https://doi.org/10.17605/OSF.IOF85QJ.

Stanek, Łukasz. *Architecture in Global Socialism: Eastern Europe, West Africa, and the Middle East in the Cold War*. Princeton, NJ: Princeton University Press, 2020.

Toure, Diala. *Créations architecturales et artistiques en Afrique sub-saharienne (1948–1995). Bureaux d'études Henri Chomette*. Paris: L'Harmattan, 2002.

Tradeship Publications Ltd. *The Global Cement Report*, 14th ed. Surrey, 2021.

United Nations, Department of Economic and Social Affairs. *World Population Prospects 2022: Summary of Results*. Statistical Papers—United Nations (Ser. A), Population and Vital Statistics Report. August 2022. → https://doi.org/10.18356/9789210014380.

United Nations, Department of Economic and Social Affairs. *World Urbanization Prospects: The 2018 Revision*. August 2019.
→ https://doi.org/10.18356/b9e995fe-en.

United Nations Environment Programme. *Sand and Sustainability: Finding New Solutions for Environmental Governance of Global Sand Resources*. Geneva, 2019.

United Nations Environment Programme, and Yale Center for Ecosystems + Architecture. *Building Materials and the Climate: Constructing a New Future*. Nairobi, 2023.
→ https://wedocs.unep.org/xmlui/handle/20.500.11822/43293. Accessed July 8, 2024.

Uzu, J., P. Bettinger, J. Siry, and B. Mei. "Timber Business in West Africa: A Review and Outlook." *International Forestry Review* 24, no. 2 (July 2022): 240–56.
→ https://doi.org/10.1505/146554822835629578.

Van Damme, Henri, and Hugo Houben. "Earth Concrete. Stabilization Revisited." *Cement and Concrete Research*, Report of UNEP Working Group on Low-CO2 Eco-Efficient Cement-Based Materials 114 (December 1, 2018): 90–102.
→ https://doi.org/10.1016/j.cemconres.2017.02.035.

Van der Lugt, Pablo, and Joost Vogtlander. "Life Cycle Assessment and Carbon Sequestration; the Environmental Impact of Industrial Bamboo Products." *INBAR Technical Report* 35, 2015.
→ https://doi.org/10.13140/RG.2.2.20797.46560.

White, Lyal. "The Case of Cement." In *Africans Investing in Africa: Understanding Business and Trade, Sector by Sector*, edited by Terence McNamee, Mark Pearson, and Wiebe Boer, 124–46. London: Palgrave Macmillan, 2015.
→ https://doi.org/10.1057/9781137542809_9.

World Bank Group. "GDP per Capita Growth (Annual %)—Sub-Saharan Africa."
→ https://data.worldbank.org/indicator/NY.GDP.PCAP.KD.ZG?locations=ZG. Accessed July 8, 2024.

Zhong, Xiaoyang, Mingming Hu, Sebastiaan Deetman, Bernhard Steubing, Hai Xiang Lin, Glenn Aguilar Hernandez, Carina Harpprecht, Chunbo Zhang, Arnold Tukker, and Paul Behrens. "Global Greenhouse Gas Emissions from Residential and Commercial Building Materials and Mitigation Strategies to 2060." *Nature Communications* 12, no. 1 (October 21, 2021): 6126.
→ https://doi.org/10.1038/s41467-021-26212-z.

Data References

●4

(a) United Nations, Department of Economic and Social Affairs. *World Urbanization Prospects: The 2018 Revision*. August 2019.
→ https://doi.org/10.18356/b9e995fe-en.

(b) FAOSTAT Land, Inputs and Sustainability; "Climate Change Indicators; Temperature Change on Land." Rome, 2024.
→ http://www.fao.org/faostat/en/#data/ET. Accessed July 8, 2024.

(c) World Bank Group. "GDP per Capita Growth (Annual %)—Sub-Saharan Africa," 2024.
→ https://data.worldbank.org/indicator/NY.GDP.PCAP.KD.ZG?locations=ZG. Accessed July 8, 2024.

(d) African Development Bank. "African Development Bank Statistical Data Portal," December 2023.
→ https://dataportal.opendataforafrica.org/. Accessed July 8, 2024.

(e) Andrew, Robbie M., and Glen P. Peters. "The Global Carbon Project's Fossil CO2 Emissions Dataset." Zenodo, November 21, 2023.
→ https://doi.org/10.5281/ZENODO.10177738.

●5

Agence Fran.aise de Développement. "Cement, Confronting Ecological Responsibility and Economic Imperatives" May 2011.
→ https://www.proparco.fr/en/ressources/cement-confronting-ecological-responsibility-andeconomic-imperatives. Accessed September 23, 2024.

●18

(a) Minke, Gernot. *Building with Earth: Design and Technology of a Sustainable Architecture*. Basel; Boston: Birkhäuser, 2006.

(b) Boubekeur, Sid, Vincent Rigassi, Ali Mesbah, Jean-Claude Morel, Hugo Houben, and Wilfredo Carazas. *Compressed Earth Blocks: Testing Procedures*. Brussels: CDE, 2000.
→ https://craterre.hypotheses.org/4003. Accessed September 23, 2024.

(c) Reddy, B. V. Venkatarama. *Compressed Earth Block and Rammed Earth Structures*. Springer Transactions in Civil and Environmental Engineering Ser. Singapore: Springer Singapore Pte. Limited, 2022.

(d) Rigassi, Vincent, and CRATerre-EAG. *Compressed Earth Blocks: Volume 1. Manual of Production*. Braunschweig: Vieweg, 1995.

●21

(a) Sphera Solutions GmbH, "Rammed Earth Wall" (Ökobaudat, 2022)
→ https://oekobaudat.de/OEKOBAU.DAT/datasetdetail/process.xhtml?uuid=3f9ebd47-f93e-4fee-859a-13700134ee3c&version=20.23.050&stock=OBD_2023_I&lang=de. Accessed July 8, 2024.

(b) Sphera Solutions GmbH, "Sand 0/2" (Ökobaudat, 2022)
→ https://oekobaudat.de/OEKOBAU.DAT/datasetdetail/process.xhtml?lang=en&uuid=8125026b-602d-47d5-9087-7470c457d10a&version=20.23.050. Accessed July 8, 2024.

(c) Sphera Solutions GmbH, "Cement (CEM II 32,5)" (Ökobaudat, 2022)
→ https://oekobaudat.de/OEKOBAU.DAT/datasetdetail/process.xhtml?uuid=55af842c-7d33-4d0c-b33b-ac7564e573bf&version=20.23.050&stock=OBD_2023_I&lang=de. Accessed July 8, 2024.

●52

(a) Sphera Solutions GmbH, "Rammed Earth Wall" (Ökobaudat, 2022)
→ https://oekobaudat.de/OEKOBAU.DAT/datasetdetail/process.xhtml?uuid=3f9ebd47-f93e-4fee-859a-13700134ee3c&version=20.23.050&stock=OBD_2023_I&lang=de. Accessed July 8, 2024.

(b) Sphera Solutions GmbH, "Sand 0/2" (Ökobaudat, 2022)
→ https://oekobaudat.de/OEKOBAU.DAT/datasetdetail/process.xhtml?lang=en&uuid=8125026b-602d-47d5-9087-7470c457d10a&version=20.23.050. Accessed July 8, 2024.

(c) Sphera Solutions GmbH, "Cement (CEM II 32,5)" (Ökobaudat, 2022),
→ https://oekobaudat.de/OEKOBAU.DAT/datasetdetail/process.xhtml?uuid=55af842c-7d33-4d0c-b33b-ac7564e573bf&version=20.23.050&stock=OBD_2023_I&lang=de. Accessed July 8, 2024.

(d) Thinkstep, "Reinforcement Steel Wire" (Ökobaudat, 2019)
→ https://www.oekobaudat.de/OEKOBAU.DAT/datasetdetail/process.xhtml?lang=en&uuid=e9ae96ee-ba8d-420d-9725-7c8abd06e082&version=20.19.120. Accessed July 8, 2024.

(e) Thinkstep, "Application Coating Silicone Paint" (Ökobaudat, 2019)
→ https://www.oekobaudat.de/OEKOBAU.DAT/datasetdetail/process.xhtml?lang=en&uuid=815fb8f6-04cc-494d-ab6b-1b6eae98bfca&version=20.19.120. Accessed July 8, 2024.

(f) Gu, Lei, Yufeng Zhou, Tingting Mei, Guomo Zhou, and Lin Xu. "Carbon Footprint Analysis of Bamboo Scrimber Flooring—Implications for Carbon Sequestration of Bamboo Forests and Its Products." *Forests* 10, no. 1 (January 2019): 51.
→ https://doi.org/10.3390/f10010051.

Image Credits

All image rights by **Project Mako e.V.** and NiokoBâti GIE

Acknowledgments

As this manual shows, building with earth is not a one-person job; the works featured in this book as well as the produced knowledge are the results of a collaboration of many actors: Alexander Duerr, Christian Gaeth, Fode Ba, Issa Diallo, Jakob Krauss, Micha Kretschmann, Mouhamadou Moctar Ba, Ousmane Ba, and Thierno Dabo are permanent members of Studio Suddo Neuve. Success and failure have shaped this collective over the past seven years, transforming an initial interest in sustainable building into a physical manifestation of a growing regenerative material culture in Mako, Senegal.

Our work was influenced and shaped by the many people who have dedicated their lives to earth building and who have shared their knowledge with us, knowingly and unknowingly; without these exchanges our intervention would not have been possible.

Both then and now, many individuals and organizations have helped our work with their minds, hands, and donations; this work would not be possible without this support. We would like to thank:

Abdourakhmane Diallo
Adama Diallo
Alanus University
Alexander Jerosch-Herold
Amadou Diallo
Américain
Anil Algan
Anna Rubbo
Dr. Annette Julius
Prof. Dr. Anooradha Siddiqi
Bano Ba
Bayfall
Caterina Costi
ClayTec Lehmbaustoffe GmbH
Columbia University
David Janotta
Doris Kleilein
Doudou Deme
Emeraude Montelus
Fode Kante
Frederic Hormesch
German Federal Ministry for Economic Cooperation and Development (BMZ)
Hans-Jürgen Gäth
Hartmut and Birgit Zantopp
Hawa Tini Diallo
Ibrahima Diallo
Ibrahima Diey
Ideal Fleet Management GmbH & Co. KG
James Wallen
Jerome Bindia
Jonathan Schwestka
Dr. Julia Apitsch-Haack
Dr. Lamine Diallo
Maçon Ba
Mamadou Ba
Marie Diallo
Marly Diallo
Prof. Matthew Sisal
Mawdo Cissokho
Natalie Tischler
Oumar Diallo
Prof. Dr. Patricia Culligan
Prof. Dr. Philipp Misselwitz
Ruben Tsangaris
Schmitz Stiftungen
Serigne Gassama
Seydou Cissakho
Dr. Stefanie Richters
Prof. Swen Geiss
Theresa Hartherz
Tidiane Ba
Ulderup Stiftung
Virserums Konsthall
Zakaria Camara
and many more ...

We offer a sincere thank you to Bauhaus Earth for giving our work a platform by including us in this series.

Imprint

A work by Studio Suddo Neuve —Collective for Earth Building in Mako, Senegal
https://www.studio-sn.earth

Conceptualized, written, and illustrated by Christian Gaeth and Micha Kretschmann

Published as part of the *Bauhaus Earth Manual* series
https://www.bauhauserde.org
contact@bauhauserde.org

Editors: Alan Organschi and Philipp Misselwitz
Editorial direction: Rosa Hanhausen
Copyediting: Christen Jamar
Proofreading: Christen Jamar
Design and setting: Ondine Pannet, Marie Schuster, Bureau Est
Typefaces: Greed by Displaay, Kleisch by Chiachi Chao
Lithography: Bild1Druck
Production: Susanne Rösler, jovis
Project management: Theresa Hartherz, jovis

Printed in the European Union

For questions about General Safety Product Regulation please contact *productsafety@degruyterbrill.com*.

Bibliographic information published by the Deutsche Nationalbibliothek: the Deutsche Nationalbibliothek lists this publication in the Deutsche Nationalbibliografie; detailed bibliographic data are available on the internet at *http://dnb.d-nb.de*.

jovis Verlag
Genthiner Straße 13
10785 Berlin

www.jovis.de

jovis books are available worldwide in select bookstores.
Please contact your nearest bookseller or visit *www.jovis.de* for information concerning your local distribution.

ISSN 2943-5528
ISBN 978-3-98612-145-7 (softcover)
ISBN 978-3-98612-146-4 (e-book)